Overstanding the G.A.M.E.
GETTING ABOVE THE MIS-EDUCATION

THE Ultimate Cheat Code to LEVEL UP & WIN
in YOUR RELATIONSHIP with YOUR ~~Child~~ Gamer

SHARTIA "LOVE" JONES

Overstanding the G.A.M.E.

Copyright © 2024 by Shartia "Love" Jones

All rights reserved. Printed in the United States of America. No part of this publication may be reproduced, distributed, or transmitted in any form or by any means, including photocopying, recording, or other electronic or mechanical methods, without the prior written permission of the publisher, except in the case of brief quotations embodied in critical reviews and certain other noncommercial uses permitted by copyright law. For more information on purchases in bulk or speaking events, please contact:

SHE PUBLISHING LLC or Shartia "Love" Jones.

The views and opinions expressed in this book are solely those of the author and do not necessarily reflect the views of the publisher. The publisher makes no representations or warranties regarding the accuracy, applicability, or completeness of the content and assumes no responsibility for any actions taken based on this work.

For information contact:

info@shepublishingllc.com
www.shepublishingllc.com

MUNSTER, INDIANA

INDIANAPOLIS, INDIANA

ISBN: 978-1-964061-24-5

Edited by Johanna Marie, Owner of Journey JoEsque LLC.
Joesquejourneystudios.com
And
Shartia "Love" Jones

Cover inspiration and design by Nabin

Forward by James Tate, III
Scripture quotations from The Holy Bible, English Standard Version. ESV® Text Edition: 2016. Copyright © 2001 by Crossway Bibles, a publishing ministry of Good News Publishers. Used by permission. All rights reserved.

Disclaimer

This book, *Overstanding the G.A.M.E.*, is intended solely for informational and thought-provoking purposes. The author is not a licensed medical doctor, therapist, psychologist, or professional counselor. The ideas, theories, and suggestions presented here are based on the author's personal insights and creative perspectives. They are not meant to replace professional medical, psychological, or legal advice.

Readers should consult qualified professionals for specific concerns, diagnoses, or treatment related to their mental, physical, or emotional health. The author disclaims any liability arising directly or indirectly from the use or application of the material within this book.

Table of Contents

Dedication i
Acknowledgements iii
Foreword vii
Introduction 1

Part 1: First Person Shooter (FPS).. 7
Level 1: The Start Up Overstanding Your Child, Gamer 8
Level 2: The Introduction Overstanding Your Role in This Game of Life 22
Level 3: GAME Loading… The History of Gaming and Overstanding the Game Ratings 35
Level 4: The Main Game Overstanding the HP's (Health Points) 54

Part 2: "Git Gud"! ("Get Good")!.. 68
Level 5: Overstanding the XP's G.A.M.E. MODE: SEL 70
Level 6: G.A.M.E. Mode - Skill-Check Take the Pre-Quiz! 113
Level 7: G.A.M.E. Mode - Affirm Team Affirmations 120
Level 8: G.A.M.E. Story Mode - THE FINALE Your Story; Your LEVEL 127
Notes and Reflections 133
Your Story, Your Level: Your Conclusion Take the Post-Quiz!........... 137

Part 3: **139**
I. Bibliography 141
II. Glossary... 144
III. Learning Terms.. 148
IV. Overstanding the G.A.M.E. Theories/Practices/Terms 150
V. S.M.A.R.T. Goals Summary 155
VI. S.M.A.R.T. Goals Intricately Defined................................. 156
VII. My Final Appreciation and Words for You, The Winner!............. 160
VIII. About the Author 161

Dedication

My Sun and My Moon,

This is the third book that my amazing and phenomenal son has inspired me to write. Of course, I am dedicating this book to him. It is because of him that I have learned, and through our experiences gained insight that I am going to share with the world. Sun, you have taught Mommy so much. I appreciate you and thank God for your existence. You have no idea how much I watch you, how much I cry and pray; While hoping I am making proper choices regarding you. Yet, when I see you, I know that amidst all my concerns about getting it wrong as your mom, I have certainly done one thing right. That one thing was helping to create you. You do your best and press through every obstacle while remaining a 'Principal Scholar.' You are brilliant, handsome, creative, talented, and so much more.

Psalm 127:3
Behold, children are a gift of the LORD, the fruit of the womb is a reward. *(The Holy Bible, English Standard Version. ESV)*

Son, I love you from the bottom of my heart to the moon and back, and I hope you know this. Continue to be who you are forever and always. Always reach to *overstand* things in life! You've taught me so much and continue to do so. We have come so far as it relates to me *Overstanding the G.A.M.E.* Stepping out of my comfort zone provided me with the opportunity to witness a version of education I wasn't privy to. Thank you for welcoming me into your world of gaming. I am grateful to you for trusting me and for sharing your space with me.

I also want to thank you for your continued patience, as I am still learning. Our laughter, jokes, communication, and your ability to teach me new things are greatly appreciated. You have taught me a deep lesson about *things* not always being the way they seem. You, and many other children are learning key characteristics, practices, and life lessons while playing the game.

On March 26, 2021, my life changed forever. I believe the result of this book will bless families and communities across the world. As I conclude this dedication and continue my love for you, I just want to leave the following words on this page for you:

> "Sun, always rely on God and your core instinct. When I am gone, know that I will ALWAYS be with you… in your heart. You'll feel me… I will be close. You and I are linked forever, EVER!

-Con Amor Siempre,

Mommy

Acknowledgements

Let's just say that during my final read through, I am OVER-emotional. I am so grateful to *God* for putting this message on my heart to share with you. God, (insert a deep breath here) is truly the author and finisher of my faith! I am grateful for the grace given during the tiresome and trying moments of this journey. I am also thankful for the *fresh wind* after the late nights and early mornings spent working on my newest *Baby*. I am forever grateful for God's faithfulness and guidance. My SUN (JT3)... Oh my, I could not have completed this without you. You have truly been amazing! (I know I was bugging you beyond measure). Thank you for believing in YOU, in ME and in OUR project! I will bounce between Sun and Son throughout this text, either way, I am referring to you. I appreciate you for supporting me along the way. Thank you for being the brightest star in my world Sun. I love you more than LOVE.

Florence Watkins (Lil Mama/Floyd Watkins Sr.-Grandparents) -Grandma, I love you so much. Thank you for our *Girly Talks,* your love and for praying for me without ceasing/Granddaddy I miss and love you so much. -Blanche Jones, Sr. and Adline Jones (My Nana and Paw-Paw who are in Heaven), I love you both. Thank you for watching over us (especially Daddy). I pray that I make you proud. -To my immediate family, I love you so much and I promise to spread this love more! My Father (J. Jones.) -I love you so much Daddy. Thank you for everything. I am listening and learning, I promise. #DaddysGirl, My Mother (G. Watkins-Jones.) - I adore you Mommy. You are truly the best Mommy ever. Thank you for everything. You and your love are so beautiful. Thank you for giving me your huge heart. #MommysBaby, My Sisters, E. Hammond, J. Johnson) - I love y'all to the moon and back. I am blessed to have you both as sisters. #ASistersLove, My Nieces (A. Hammond, J. Johnson., and S. Johnson) -

You all are so Beautiful, smart, and AMAZING! Thank you for showing me so much LOVE. I am so proud of you all and I cannot wait to spoil you more #TíaTiaLove 4-EvaEva!

Elijah I., I remember brainstorming with you about this concept, thank you for being you, you are brilliant, and I appreciate the push! Stacy K., you have been a blessing and a loyal friend. Your prayers and kind words are always on time. Thank you from the bottom of my heart. I would like to thank S. Burton and The S.H.E. Publishing Family -The Love. The Support. The Family. The Push. The Belief. I love y'all beyond words. We are in this for life! My Editor: Johanna Mason - Oh my God, you really saw, felt and believed. I adore you and I am so grateful for your gift. Thank you for handling everything with such grace and professionalism. You are a blessing. To My Beta Readers: Tiffany J., Amanda P., Latoya B. You truly saw the vision in its rawest form and gave me so much encouragement. Words cannot describe my gratitude to those of you who played such a huge role in this very necessary movement. Your words pushed me to continue when I was not sure if I was being as expressive as I needed to be. You pulled the passion and the message out of my first draft, I needed that. I hope you like your surprise! Turn the book over. 😊

To My Pastor Rev. Trunell D. Felder, Marlene McDonald, The Administration Team and my entire New Faith International Baptist Church family - You all have pushed me, prayed for me, supported and believed in me. I am forever grateful to you. Thank you for seeing me and for accepting me for who I am (flaws and all). Rev. Felder spoke this Sunday and there were some specific words that pierced and resonated with my soul. He said, "The material for your miracle is in your hand." With tears in my eyes, I passionately believe this for myself and for anyone who holds (or listens to) this guide. New Faith Family, I am forever grateful to you all. "*I love y'all and ain't nothing you can do about it.*" 😊

To Dionna Reynolds -Thank you for believing in me and for supporting me in my entrepreneurial dreams. You truly are an *Angel* in human form. Thank you for being so Beautiful. Your kindness is forever embedded in my heart. I love you forever!

To My Sister Friends: L. Johnson, J. Reyes, T. Stovall, Q. Wells, A. West, K. Potts, S. Romia, T. Jones, J. Moore, A. Harvey, T. White, T. Hale, J. Radcliffe, V. Bullie, K. Mills, R. Rivera, T. Clasberry, A. White, S. Booker, D. Jones, B. Eatherly, A. Moore, F. Hoyne, T. Brown, L. Martin, D. Barefield, E. Hardeway, S. Wise, L. Roberts, K. Jayashari, M. Bussie, A. George, A. Jones, S. Morehead and T. Harrison… Each of you have consistently shown up and out for me these last few years and in great capacities. We may not talk all the time, but whenever we connect it is genuine. You have love for me, intentions to see me prosper, and you are authentic. Most importantly, you are there when I need you. I can only hope I have offered the same support to you. I love you all so much, I can barely type! I love y'all to the moon and back. To: The 1st Love Jones Alliance; Self-Love -Class Edition Graduates: Toya, Danielle, Kasira, Ann and Torrie. I love you and I am so proud of you. Thank you for trusting me to teach and share my passion. I look forward to what the future has for our Team! Y'all are forever embedded in my heart for your loyalty and press.

Tantra Stovall, I love you so much and I thank God for you. Your presence in my life is appreciated beyond words. You have been there in ways that supersede kindness, patience, love, and acceptance. Your sistership means so much to me. I am here forever and always.

#Promise #CaramelAndMochaChronicles forever and always…

To My brothers (C. Lyons, A. Walton, and M. Chavers) - I appreciate y'all for putting up with your Sis, I know I am a handful. I truly thank you for being there when I need y'all most. Thank you for loving me and for caring for me in the most organic ways, I love you! To my Mentees: K. Hill and K. Phillips, the way y'all show up for me!!! #Tears, I love you and I thank you for allowing me to love on y'all too. There is greatness in store for you both! I am here, always.

To M. Williams, R. Willy, Q. Parks, R. Johnson, B. James, and D. Butler, thank you for caring for me and for your support. I hope I return the love that you have given me. You are truly adored.

J. Tate Jr. -Thank you for partnering with me in this 'Parenting Thing,' you & Kai are a blessing.

To: *All Jazzed Up, 360 Entertainment, Trugains Fitness, Detoxx Products, That's a Cake, TB Lash and Beauty, Manifest Salon Suites, Bella B's, A & S Divine Healthcare, Pendulum Ink, Poise Beauty*, My *L.E.A.R.N.* Family (*Morehead, Beach, Harper, Waters, etc.*), -I thank you and your brand/organization for believing in me and mine. #Muah -I love you to the moon and back.

"It is only up from here." - Mikey (Our handsome Angel in Heaven you are missed greatly. We love you) ... and you are right, it is only up from here. Thank you for watching over your Mom and Sister. Until we meet again…

To Everyone else who had an influence on my journey to finishing this book and encouraged me along the way, you mean so much to me and I am grateful to you on so many levels. Tears beyond tears! I may not have listed you personally, but you are in my heart forever. I love you and I will put you in the next book or the 2nd Edition if you were missed. Hugs and Blessings.

Foreword

Coming from "Love" Jones' son, this book is truly a masterpiece. My mother and I's relationship has been growing for years mainly because of how, *overstanding* she is with my hobbies and habits. This book takes a deep dive into one of my main hobbies, gaming. She helps others to analyze video games from a gamer's perspective. Then, she shares details from her parental and educational viewpoints. My mom crafts a way to bridge all three vantage points together. This bridge is an intelligent and creative step towards true *overstanding*.

This book can be placed in the hands of anyone in the gaming world who desires to understand, I mean *overstand*. It is a fun and intellectual experience to read the whole way through. Overstanding the game can be difficult at first, but when you take a deeper look into it, things get intriguing and alluring. As her son, I am proud to see my mother write a book on such a wonderful topic that I thoroughly enjoy. It is a detrimental and excellent move for a loved one to *Overstand the G.A.M.E.* I hope you enjoy it, learn, and build better relationships with your gamer, parents, guardians, and loved ones in your own way.

- James III (JT3)

Introduction

From *Gameboy* and *PlayStation* to *LeapFrog* and CD-ROM games, we have all encountered or observed gaming on some level. One of the top ten games played in the world right now is *Minecraft*. You may have heard of this one. Perhaps you have also heard of *Fortnite*, *NBA 2K*, *Roblox*, *Call of Duty* and *Grand Theft Auto* (*GTA*). You might be familiar with other popular games such as: *Apex Legends*, The *Super Mario* game series, and EA Sports games. Video games have been around for decades, and have evolved from the arcade form, to handhelds, and beyond. We will delve deeper into the history of gaming later. Be that as it may, I want you to think about these key milestones as it pertains to gaming.

The very first video game was called SPACEWAR, and it was created in 1962 by MIT student hobbyists. However, the first consumer video game was *Computer Space,* released in 1971, followed by *Pong*, the iconic arcade game. The first home console was the *Magnavox Odyssey*. There were so many games and gaming devices released between the 1970s and the early 2000s that you probably have your own favorites and memories of watching others engage in the new hands-on technology. One may even remember the *1983 Video Game Crash*. This was a large recession surrounding video gaming due to low quality games, the home computer boom and a console price war. *The Nintendo Entertainment System (NES)* brought the gaming world back to life and paved the way for the consoles our children currently utilize. The gaming systems and features have gotten even more realistic and advanced over the years. Consider the games you can play right from your phone, the *Wii* games, and virtual reality games. While the evolution and development of gaming is quite fascinating, I found myself becoming less impressed with its impact on my son.

My Son loves playing several video games. Long ago we used to play *Wii Sports* and other interactive games on the *Nintendo Wii* together. My Sun loved the idea of using the remote as a pointer and point of reference while participating in the games. It truly was enjoyable and interactive! We were always impressed regarding its ability to detect movement. Nonetheless, it had been an exceedingly long time since we engaged in playing video games, and the **Time on Game** wasn't so time-consuming back then.

Times were certainly different. I grew up playing a few games too. However, my favorite games to play were *PacMan, Super Mario Brothers, Galaga* and *Contra*. With this significant difference, I wasn't sure how we would connect in this space. I knew he would laugh at the way the games I played looked aesthetically. I was so confused about how to relate to my child while he was glued to the game. Hence my reason for authoring this book. I thought to myself, I cannot be the only person asking themselves various questions surrounding gaming. Questions like, "How do I get some time with my son who only wants to play the game? Why is he screaming at this television? Did he eat today or leave his lunch on the table again?" First, I thought getting angry, putting my foot down, and taking away the game were the correct choices.

After thinking about my goal, I realized that getting angry and taking away the game may not be the best approach. My goal was for us to bond together, not to place an even wider wedge in between us. I wanted to find a solution and I wanted to ensure I was doing my part. I was not only a concerned and active parent, I was also an educator and child advocate. I have taught elementary school, middle school, high school, and collegiate level courses. While drafting this book, I was in educational leadership as the Dean of Students for a school in Chicago, IL.

As a mommy, a life coach, and at the time a school dean, it was difficult for me to feel disconnected from my son as he developed over time. This was especially difficult for me to digest because I was able to connect with other children his age. (I maintained connections with my scholars from the school community and others from my previous speaking events too).

Honestly, I just wanted to be involved. I wanted to be able to communicate with my son without frustration. I will admit this too, I also wanted to be a cool mom; one he'd sometimes want around during *gametime*. So, how would I accomplish my goals? Why did I feel so helpless, frustrated, and disappointed regarding the distance between my son's gaming experiences and I? In my mind, I thought I was educated. Maybe I wasn't…?

This was the defining moment. The moment I learned that I needed to ***Get Above the Mis-Education*** of the game and get a grip on my original way of thinking.

Q: WHO IS THIS BOOK FOR & HOW DO I USE IT???

A: This book is for anyone who feels they are gradually disconnecting from a gamer in their life. You are *battling* and losing the fight for your relationship to the lure of the game. This book is for couples, friends, school leaders, church organizations, non-for-profit organizations, and beyond. The vision is for us to have and live in a more cohesive world where we seek to *overstand* one another. This should cause us to embrace our differences in love, while becoming better communicators. According to History.com on Jun 10, 2019, Today, video games make up a one hundred-billion-dollar global industry, and nearly two-thirds of American homes have household members who play video games regularly. So, I know there are many engaging in video gaming activities and at a costly price. However, this stimulating activity does not have to cost us our relationships. To mitigate continued pain, I charge you to *overstand* the gaming process.

I strongly suggest you read the book and follow along in the order it is written. However, if you need to bounce around so you can use distinct parts of the book in a way that fits into your life, please do so. This interactive reference guide will be here for you in the capacity that you need it. Once you review the *Table of Contents*, you'll want to organize your time, engagement activities, and communication efforts to the best of your ability.

Bonus: You will see **<u>Light-Bulb Questions</u>** throughout the book! Use them. They are meant to be conversation starters: Feel free to use the potential conversation starter questions with your child, there is even space for you to create your own!

Bear in mind that timing is everything. Be sure to pray/meditate and focus on the desired outcome for you and your gamer. Sometimes we dive right into things without preparation. Either way, please give yourself some grace as you begin this path. A helpful tip is to use the Light-Bulb conversation starters during dinner, lunch, or family time. You'll have various options while processing each level of this journey! There are **Light-Bulb Moments**, **Keys/Cheat Codes, Interactive Reflections**, and **real** game references throughout the book to keep you connected, introducing you to each level of **<u>Overstanding the G.A.M.E.</u>** You will also have access to *Vocabulary* (Bolded Words and Theories) and *Basic Education Standards* so you can make helpful connections to the gaming experience, expanding your learning from an academic point of view. This is an educational resource, of course there is a glossary at the end. As an added bonus you will find the *S.M.A.R.T.* Goals breakdown, team affirmations and a quiz to take before (and after) reading this guide to help measure your progress.

This is more than a book; it is also an interactive reference tool and guide. You will be asked for your thoughts, and I am hoping you are able to create safe spaces for you and your gamer within these pages. In *Level 8; Your Story, Your Level,* you will find reserved spaces to jot down your notes, thoughts, ideas, plans, etc. on the pages titled, "**<u>Notes and Reflections</u>**." Whatever comes to mind is perfectly okay. Allow yourself *room* to be YOU. If you feel like jotting down notes in the margins, highlighting and underlining ideas that speak to you, do that. This is your space, and you are welcome here!

Bonus: Each family is different. Our various dynamics are what make our world so beautiful and colorful. Just be sure to create S.M.A.R.T. Goals and prioritize them. Schedule intentional time with your gamer, just as you schedule other important things that need to get accomplished.

As you become intentional with your time, you will learn how to power up, stand up and level up as you win with your child! I have packed this book with information for you and anyone else who is unsure of where to start. You will be able to use this as a guide if you have never played a video game, are an avid player or if you play every now and then. You will learn various things about gaming that will be helpful. You may need to know what careers are out there for your child if they decide to take gaming more seriously. You may need to *overstand* what your child could be learning while playing the game right now. You may need to *overstand* some of the language your child uses while playing the game and what those terms mean. You can also use this guide if you aren't aware of how to foster a relationship with your child who is addicted to their game. Your relationship with your child can improve if you stay the course and continue to learn.

While there is a special emphasis on relationships with children, my goal is to assist you in building a more profound relationship with your gamer. This reference guide is here to assist parents/guardians, school leaders and those in relationships too. Simply replace the word child and gamer with significant other when you see it or hear it. I have had conversations with many couples, and you were also on my mind while creating this interactive tool. *Overstanding the G.A.M.E.* is meant to be a resource for you as well! My goal is to initiate opportunities to foster Love and exercise Growth. In conclusion, if you have a gamer in your life, keep reading to get involved and prepare yourself for *Overstanding the G.A.M.E.* At the end of the day, Love on your gamer. It is significant to practice this act of kindness. Keep them coming home and in other *safe spaces* with LOVE. Remember to engage and always G.A.M.E. (***Get Above the Mis-Education)!***

Part 1

First Person Shooter (FPS)

Seeing through Your Gamer's Eyes
& Interacting in Their World

Level 1: The Start Up

Overstanding Your Child, Gamer

OVERSTANDING:

So, what is, *Overstanding the G.A.M.E.?* What does **Getting A**bove *the* **M**is-**E**ducation (*G.A.M.E.*), mean? I cannot wait to tell you. Let's start by defining the words themselves. According to Webster's Dictionary, the word *overstand* means, "to keep on a navigational course beyond (a mark)". Webster's definition means to extend beyond a desired or pre-determined goal. It reminds me of the expression we often use to describe an over achiever such as, "going the extra mile". However, I don't believe that *overstanding* the game is just overachieving or being extra. May I add to our understanding here by breaking it down some more? Let's start with a simpler word within the term, *over*. The word 'over' means to cross a barrier or to intervene, according to Webster's Dictionary. The Etymology, origin of the word, is an old English term translated from the German word 'ubar' meaning, 'beyond', like the Latin word super, and the Greek word hyper. When you think of the word 'over' this engages our minds to operate from an elevated level of consciousness, to cross *over* socially established barriers to our understanding. Operating from "above" is powerful. So, I want you to "OVER" stand, **Getting Above the Mis-Education** (*G.A.M.E.*) regarding video gaming and those who play. We are not beneath anything, nor are we seeking to find more clarity from scratching the surface. Seeking to *overstand* rather than just understand, especially when it comes to the ones we love, should forever be our goal. It will enhance the quality of our relationships and our lives!

In February of 2020, our lives changed forever. Mommies, daddies, grandparents, guardians, school personnel, business organizations, everyone and everything changed. We all had to endure and embrace a *shut-in home life* during the COVID-19 pandemic. As families were instructed to stay indoors, finding new ways to spend time at home was more important than ever. New hobbies were formed and many of our children gravitated towards gaming. There were few options for children to socialize during this time, and when I asked my son why he played the game so much he said, "It just makes me feel better Mom." Gaming was a way to cope with all that he was enduring. When I learned to unpack my child's reality and the importance of it, I started to look at the gaming situation differently. I also needed to figure out what part I played in his gaming, and what strategy was going to be most useful to my son. Little did I know, gaming was already a big part of both our lives. The game impacted me on various levels.

The first level of impact started with the point of purchase. After purchasing this gaming system, it wasn't long before it began to drive me crazy. I ordered it in advance and stood in line for hours to bring home this new *device* and its accompanying game. This dynamic duo kept my child busy and insanely involved. The amount of time my child spent on the game, the intense energy spent yelling or getting frustrated with his friends as he played, seemed to be beyond comprehension (and my emotional capacity, if I am honest). His lack of attention to other things was increasing. My child was missing meals, slacking in chores, study time, family moments etc. because he was so enthralled with the game. I thought to myself, "What could I do as a parent to find some sort of peace with this situation?" I was *over* it!

Does this situation sound familiar? Have you felt this way before? Does it apply to what you have going on with your gamer? Do you desire to have a better relationship with your gamer?

Well, I'd like to help. If you nodded your head or agreed with any of those questions, I *totally* feel you. It felt like I was in a different space mentally and emotionally. I was getting so frustrated and oftentimes would just say, "Get off the game. I am sick of it, and the yelling, and ALL OF IT." After expressing this countless times, I decided to stop and take a step back to view things from my son's lens. I settled into a moment of silence after much prayer and decided to try something different. I put myself in my son's shoes and focused on him. Removing myself and my frustrations from this equation was extremely helpful. This activity led me to thoughts about life as it is today and where we *all* are right now in this world.

We are living in times that we never thought we would see. Who would have thought we would experience the COVID-19 pandemic, people storming The White House, so much hate, crime, famine, cars that drive themselves, snow in Texas (U.S.A.), natural disasters, war on peace, internal and personal battles, etc. I don't know about you, but I certainly wouldn't have *ever* guessed. Before we pass off judgment and ignore what our youth have experienced in the last few years, let's think deeper for a moment.

I taught online, planned virtual events and drive-by graduations during the pandemic. I was highly engaged and very intentional about calling my scholars superheroes! Why? Well, our youth have been quite resilient and strong. They've pushed through fear and the unknown. I am aware because they shared their fears and concerns with me. Most had to wear masks for years and their childhood experiences have been altered significantly. During key moments when they wanted and needed to be social, they could not. They attended classes and graduations from their homes or engaged in drive-by celebrations. They probably witnessed their parents and guardians working from home, maintaining, and coping in the best ways possible. Our children stayed indoors without full understanding of what was going on and how long it would last. Life was different and they were also coping in the best ways possible.

My son's **gameplay** became an opportunity to express who he is and release stress by engaging in a different world. A virtual world that mimics in creative ways the world we actually live in. You might recognize that your child is escaping real life into another version of the real world through gaming. You might witness your child expressing themselves in a way online or virtually, that is different from who they present themselves to be in person. This is something to be curious about and to navigate through with your child. If your child is showing up differently online, I would consider what are their reasons for doing so? Are there things happening in real, physical time that are hindering their ability to feel connected to themselves? Is your child stressed by external or internal factors? What is the root cause of the change? Are they looking for a fun outlet and just want to let loose for a little while and be whoever they want, with no consequences, other than the game rules of course?

THE CHEAT CODE:

If there is one thing I have learned, it is that we must be open to learning from our youth. We need to be willing to put our egos and pride aside. Yes, we are adults. However, that doesn't mean we are experts in every area. Especially as it pertains to gaming, technology, and gadgets. Think about it, how many times has a younger person or gamer fixed something on your phone, computer, television, or other device? How many times have they connected and reconnected the WIFI? How many times have you had to ask someone else for the password to various things? Please know, it is okay to learn from our amazing scholars. When you dig deep, I am hoping you will find that today's youth have extremely vast and intelligent minds. They are a part of a true technological culture. It may be hard to admit, but times just are not the same, and things are changing at great speeds.

In life, things are all about perspective, the way we choose to look at things and what outcomes are possible. What can you do regarding your perspective to have more peace within? I've found a solution to this gaming *trigger* that may have some folks wanting to toss the gaming systems out of the window. (Please don't do that, they cost too much, LBVS). How do I know you are ready to see if these systems can fly? Well, because I was there too, before I found this first gaming relationship **Cheat Code**!

It is simpler than you might think. It is so simple that it is often overlooked. Heck, this practice went over my head for a long time, and I have twenty-five years of experience in education.

Have you figured out the answer yet? Well, let's really get down to it and let me reveal this million-dollar answer to you. The answer is **INVOLVEMENT**! Oftentimes, we just need to get involved and meet our child where they are. We often try to find common ground with our jobs, our careers, and relationships. Yet, when it comes to our children and technology, we tend to put our belief systems, old ways of thinking, and our personal theories on them. We sometimes do this without realizing they have their own mind, peer interactions, and views based on their experiences.

Getting involved in your gamer's "Game life," can be like learning another language. Once you begin to understand when and how words, phrases, and even game parts are used you can join in on the communication and overcome a lack of *overstanding*.

Light-Bulb Moment:

Q: Do you know the different terms for gaming systems or ways a game can be played? (Here is one way to answer that question).

A: Gaming systems are often called consoles. There are three types of video game consoles: home consoles, handhelds, and hybrid consoles.

Q: Do you know the different brand names of video game consoles?

A: There are five main platforms in the video gaming space: *Nintendo Switch* (is a handheld gaming system), *Microsoft Xbox*, The *Sony PlayStation,* Personal Computers (PCs) & Mobile Devices. (Special Note: I must give the *Nintendo Wii* an honorable mention. This is a gaming console my son and I played long ago. It has been named as his favorite due its universal intractability).

Q: Which one do you think is the most played? Ask your child, this can be a conversation starter for you both!

A: *PlayStation 5* and the *Xbox Series X* have gone head-to-head in competition for the most played. The *Nintendo Switch* has been played more frequently than all Sony consoles combined.

THEORY OF PARENTAL INVOLVEMENT:

Let's just say that I learned a lot by simply getting involved. I *overstand* that what is important to my Sun should at least inspire me to want to know more. On our journey, I learned, we bonded, we laughed, and he enjoyed teaching me and talking to me about what he loves. It was amazing to hear him teach with such excitement. I'd always known he was brilliant. Our interaction and observance caused me to witness the true level of intelligence he embodies. As an early childhood development scholar and experienced behavior interventionist, I try to practice the Theory of Parental Involvement as much as possible. This theory states the following: Children whose parents or parental figures are involved in their education will be more likely to develop a strong, positive sense of efficacy for successfully achieving school-related tasks than will children whose parents are not involved.

While writing, I was inspired to create a new theory by merging the Theory of Parental Involvement with my experience. This newer theory is similar but takes on a *new skin*. This skin is called the **Theory of Parental and Guardian Involvement Regarding Gaming**. It states: Children whose parents or parental figures are involved in their child's *gameplay* experiences will be more likely to build a stronger, more positive sense of overstanding, peace, and efficacy. Relationship building will offer and provide a *safe space* for all involved. These dynamics will make room for greater communication, clarity, and an *overstanding* between the child and the parent or guardian. These practices usually result in healthier relationships, fond memories, and more productive life experiences overall.

The things you choose to focus on regarding your gamer's journey are the very things that will develop and grow. It is important to internalize the work and time it will take for the *overstanding* process. Will you always feel like practicing and working towards your goal? Maybe not, change takes time and there are phases within these transitions. It may take you and your family a while to develop the habit of change; this is okay. Change can certainly be good and if we can guarantee anything in this life, it is the idea of change.

Let's start to get away from the, 'I Wasn't Like That' way of thinking. That theory will have us stuck in understanding versus *overstanding*. Haven't our lives been altered as parents and guardians, nurturers, teachers, etc.? It is pertinent to have a growth mindset approach to this experience. As adults, we must always remain teachable. Continuing to learn and develop through adulthood is as equally important as the responsibility to guide and lead our children. We must be open to learning, even if our lessons come from a toddler, adolescent, teenager, or young adult.

THE END-GAME:

Getting involved can also mean learning about how the world is impacted by video games and the gaming industry itself. For example, learning facts about how much you can make in the gaming profession might surprise you. PayScale, an online database dedicated to compensation research and job pay trends tells us how much the average gamer can make in the industry. The average annual salary for a game coder in the United States is $58,952. However, salaries for game coders vary considerably based on the level of experience, employer, and location. According to PayScale:

> Video game programmers earned an average yearly salary of $63,400 as of July 2022, with the top 10% making $90,0003. Game Developers make an average of $91,009. The average video game coder makes $76,000 per year, with the lowest ten percent of earners making $39,000 annually and the highest ten percent of earners making over $123,000. (Average Video Game Programmer Salary, Payscale.com)

I encourage you to conduct your own research on the *Professional Gaming YouTubers/TikTokers* your children, scholars, or family members follow and watch. Look up the games they are playing and read the reviews, really dive deep into this. I promise you will find out more than you thought you would. Knowledge is power and it is important that you make yourself aware; arm yourself with knowledge and differing views. Filling yourself with knowledge and learning more will surely help you Power Up!

Broaden your perspective so you can stay connected to your child and continue to engage in conversations that interest your child. You can also attend gaming conferences and other events that support gamers. Search for them on the web, they are everywhere. I was able to take my son to the *2024 Dream Con Event*. *Dream Con* is an anime and gaming convention that started back in 2018. The experience was truly Epic. The breakout sessions and panel discussions were very informative too. Topics ranged from "Worldbuilding: Guide to Writing" to "Anime and Mental Health: Main Character Energy Saved My Life…" and beyond! My Sun was so excited and even got a chance to meet his favorite YouTuber, *Berleezy* (@berleezy)!

We truly had an amazing time and are looking forward to the *2025 Dream Con Event*.

Honestly, there is a lesson for everyone embedded in the core of this world of gaming. How much research did you do prior to getting the first game or gaming system you bought? Most likely you purchased it as a gift and simply wanted to make your child happy. You didn't know you were going to have to determine your own relationship to the game, navigate your child's potential excessive *gameplay*, and exude patience for the rest of the gaming experiences that were to come.

Your child may not have been prepared for the level of patience they were going to need while learning a gaming system either. Your child is going to have to learn to play their game of choice and may fail many times prior to succeeding. These are also moments that I love! These are called *teachable moments*. Oh my, I have had many of these on this *G.A.M.E.* journey. Although these games are virtual and aren't physical, practice is still key as with anything we want to become great at in life.

Now that you have gotten through the first level, I want you to unpack, or to start to unbox what you do know and what you want to learn about your gamer and the game.

FPS TIME!
(First Person Shooter, Time!)

Seeing through Your Gamer's Eyes & Interacting in Their World

Goal 1: To help you build a maturing relationship with your child as you learn more about gaming and the developmental state of your gamer. You have the potential to excel in any Game of Life scenario… As long as you embrace LOVE, remain open to learning and strive to deeply OVERSTAND.

Why is this important?

Meeting children where they are is so important. Getting on their level, getting engaged, finding interest in what they are interested in provides a completely different level of *overstanding*. Listening to my son, hearing his reasons and his 'why' made all the difference in the world. My son was so excited to share all he knew with me, even though some of it went way over my head. He was probably just happy that I (finally) wasn't speaking negatively regarding his, sometimes intense, gaming. Instead, I wanted to be involved and *overstand* his experience. When we have consistent communication, aspire to build, and are dedicated to *overstanding*, our relationships improve. This was all part of my journey towards ***Getting Above the Mis-Education***. If I can do it, you can too! It is time for you to LEVEL UP.

Light-Bulb Questions: Ask your child, "Why do you enjoy playing the game so much?" *Be open to their answer*. Let them respond fully without interrupting them.

Ask them, "What else do you enjoy doing that gives you that same *enjoyable* feeling?" Ask your child, "Would you be willing to teach me more about the games you play?"

Special Note:

- Your Gamer may play with friends, other times they may play with an artificial intelligence function. There are also other characters in some games called Non-Playable Characters (NPCs), these characters cannot be controlled by your gamer.

Cheat Code: *INVOLVEMENT & OVERSTANDING YOUR* ~~CHILD~~, ***GAMER***

Bonus Code + Jump to **Level Six** *and take the* **Pre-Quiz***. Assess where you are right now and read the results. Write your results and any other thoughts in the "Notes and Reflections" section in* **Level Eight.** *(This way you can reference your score and previous notes and see how far you've come after reading)!*

What Light-Bulb Question(s) will you ask? (Feel free to come up with your own questions).

Date: _____ Time: _____
Place: _____

_____
_____
_____
_____
_____
_____
_____
_____
_____
_____
_____
_____
_____
_____
_____
_____
_____
_____
_____
_____
_____
_____
_____
_____
_____
_____

How did your child respond? What communication took place? How do you feel?

Date: _____ Time: _____
Place: _____

_____
_____
_____
_____
_____
_____
_____
_____
_____
_____
_____
_____
_____
_____
_____
_____
_____
_____
_____
_____
_____
_____
_____
_____
_____
_____
_____

I am so proud of you! You are taking the necessary steps to build your gaming relationship. Whether it went well in your opinion or not, what did you learn from this *teamwork* experience?

Date: _____   Time: _____
Place: _____

_____
_____
_____
_____
_____
_____
_____
_____
_____
_____
_____
_____
_____
_____
_____
_____
_____
_____
_____
_____
_____
_____
_____
_____
_____
_____

Level 2: The Introduction

*Overstanding **Your** Role in This Game of Life*

OVERSTANDING YOUR ROLE:

So far, we have taken steps toward *overstanding* our beloved gamers and have processed in level one why it's so important. We have considered what it can take to ***Get Above the Mis-Education*** and what might be driving our gamer to the game in the first place. Next, we must consider our role in this game of life. Ultimately, doing so will help us to show up in a healthier way, giving us an *overstanding* of our role in our gamer's life too. To acquire this next *cheat code* and get to level two of, *Overstanding the G.A.M.E.,* we must pause, go back to the beginning, and dig a little deeper.

I was an angry mom. That's it. That is where this portion of our story began. I didn't know how to connect with my son. Prior to this *game phase* it used to be so easy to spend time with him. We would go to the park, play board games, play basketball, ride our bikes, sit, and chat, have family time, listen to music, watch our favorite shows, visit theme parks and more. Then, *COVID-19* happened, and it seemed like all he wanted to do was play the game and talk to his friends.

In all transparency, my feelings were hurt. I felt lost. I sometimes took my lack of *overstanding* out on him by asking him to get off the game. This situation caused me to feel like a failure as a mom. I felt like a failure because I could not seem to connect with my own child. Every time he said, "I'm going to go play my game," my stomach would get into knots; "Were the previously mentioned fun experiences suddenly a lost cause?" This season of life was quite challenging for me.

I used to think, "Maybe the age gap is contributing to my lack of *overstanding*..." Perhaps the generational differences were too great, and the lack of clarity regarding the *gaming phase* was just too vast for me to *get it*. I was feeling alone, a little scared, and lost as a single mom during COVID. I was irritable and cried often during these times of confusion. (Was I losing the connection with my SUN too)?! I just did not like that feeling. The tension was thick in our home, and I didn't know what to do. It was and still is extremely important for me to feel connected to my son. Connection and relationship building are key building blocks for *safe spaces* and *overstanding*. These building blocks were certainly *missing in action*.

With each gut wrenching and slow passing day, our relationship was suffering more. (It was odd to feel like he was growing fast while the days were moving slowly). I thought we would grow closer during COVID-19, being that we were stuck inside our homes most of the time, but no. This reality had me in a constant state of concern and worry. Why did I worry? Well, as a parent, one thing I always strive to have is an open line of communication with my child. A direct line. I always want my child to feel like he can come to me, no matter what. However, this was not what we were experiencing. I could not help but think to myself, "If he isn't talking to me about things, who is he talking to?" I was feeling like a stranger in my own home, like I was invading his space and did not fit in. I had officially arrived at *that point*. Arriving at *that point* is a defined moment in time where something has occurred, and a person has reached their capacity regarding an experience. It is at this time that change of some kind usually occurs. (One of my previous mentors taught me how to identify this feeling). I am grateful because this is a defined moment, and things must change once this is realized.

I had to figure something out. My mind and heart were in an unusual space, a desperate space and it was time to wave my white flag! I had to figure out what needed to be done. After the warm tears, sleepless nights, and conversations with friends and family that really didn't lead to any *aha* moments, I did one more thing. A thing that felt like it should have been my first response. On this particular evening, while my son was playing his games two levels below, I fell to my knees, cried, and prayed. I cried myself to sleep that night. When they say, "Joy comes in the morning," it's true. Joy certainly comes in the morning! When I woke up, the answer was right in front of my face. It had always been there. It was already in me. This answer was embedded in the core of my being.

I think that sometimes we can be too close to a moment or can over analyze an experience. When we don't give it room to breathe or choose to trust the process, we can find ourselves in a head space that we would normally avoid. If I'd chosen to pause instead of worrying, perhaps I would have found peace in my heart sooner. Well, better late than never is the *positive aspect* I'm going to go with. I am so glad I got my answer and decided to lean into what I received.

Now that I had the answer, I began to feel anxious and nervous. I thought, "Was this answer as profound as I felt it was? What if he didn't like this idea?" I knew what I believed, but of course, the "what ifs" surfaced. Thoughts such as, "What if it doesn't work, and I'm sent back to square one again? Would I feel rejected? Would this rejection be too heavy for me?" Being that I am someone who feels fear and still pushes anyway, I chose to press on. I decided to think intentionally and whispered to myself, "But, what if it DOES WORK?" So, I did what was in my heart to do.

March 26, 2021, I will remember this day forever. Although we were still pressing through COVID and its remnants, it was a warm and beautiful spring day. The breeze was flowing through our home on this peaceful afternoon. The sun was shining brightly through our living room windows, and I was blessed with a powerful feeling of confidence. I felt the energy and adrenaline flowing through my body; I felt like that day was the day! I'd just finished my workout and made a late lunch. I was about to eat, but of course, he wanted me to wait and leave his meal on the counter because he was playing the game. This time, I decided against making any, "forgetting to eat" references or smart comments after he asked me to leave the food on the counter. Instead, I sat down, said my grace, and started to eat. As I was eating, I said with a shaky, yet as bold as I could muster up type of voice, "Wwwhat are you playing?"

He was very engaged while playing, but I noticed the look of *shock* on his face. I also felt confusion, due to his body language. He turned around slowly, looked at me with a perplexed gaze, and said, *"Overwatch."* He turned to refocus and finally said to his friend, "Hey, let's split up this time." I waited in anticipation of his next physical or verbal response. He continued to chat with his friend. So, instead of giving up, I became an engaged observer. I figured out instantly that while he is playing the game, he can't guess if one gamer knows what another gamer is going to do. They *must* communicate frequently and often just in case plans change. If they do change, they must decide what strategy they will use to accomplish the goals of that level or game.

Wow, I was learning already. I used to be frustrated about the noise and over-communication. Yet, I soon realized that as with anything and anyone else, it is through over communication that they accomplish anything together. Communication is key. So, I took a deep breath and casually continued to ask questions; "What are you playing, again? That looks interesting." He said, *"Overwatch."* Next, I said, "What is your job and goal, and what's going on?" … And so, it began!

My Sun said,

> A properly balanced game means having two of each of the above listed characters represented. If three people play the role of the damage team, I will play the spot that needs to be covered. The goal is to have a balanced game. I like to balance my team based on what our team's needs are. So, if we need a healer (which is most of the time) that is what I play because most gamers want to be a tank… so they can go in and do damage. I like to help, but I like playing all of them.

At this point I was hooked, engaged, and started to instantly feel connected to him and the GAME!

"Slow down so you can be healed, I am right here." That is what my son said next. I understood exactly what he meant! If the other gamer kept going in for the attack, he might have died in that game. However, once he was told to slow down so he could be healed, he was able to gain more energy and continue. The other player could have also been moving too fast, solely focused on the target, and could have died. Therefore, it is helpful to have another gamer to communicate with just in case they notice details pertaining to their survival and ultimate objective.

During this Light-Bulb conversation, my son said, "Dying to a healer is embarrassing." I said, "Aww… son, at least you tried. Healers get tired too." His reply was, "True," as he sunk into his own posture.

Wow, this hit me very differently. The fact that he wanted to be a healer and felt that dying was embarrassing meant he comprehended how important his role was on the team. It also gave me the opportunity to dive deeper and have a conversation with him surrounding emotions. We discussed thoughts and feelings that came up for him in that space, taking advantage of this *teachable moment*, just as we discussed in level one.

I let him know that in life sometimes we lose, sometimes things do not work out the way we imagined, but that we can always get back up. Heck, those with big hearts who care *a lot*, get tired and we must re-up and heal too! He *overstood*. I was so grateful we were having conversations about the game, social emotional health, and life. I was able to share personal situations I'd gone through in life including my own experiences with heartbreak. I also talked to him about mistakes and various lessons I'd learned. These conversations were very necessary and transparent moments for both of us. Our children need to know we go through things too. This level of vulnerability is a real-life example of strength and resilience. It is also evidence of how we *Stand-Up* for ourselves and our gamer. When we are honest with them, they can see that we are human, and we become relatable. This will build trust and open the door for future discussion opportunities.

Considering all of this, I had an honest mommy moment during that season of my life… There is so much happening that I must admit, I don't mind my son being inside. As much as I want him to be active, our *world* is displaying many unstable and troubling transitions. Therefore, I don't mind his desire to be in the house, if he is sure to get out and explore sometimes.

Pause.

I really want you to hear; Correction, I really want you to <u>listen</u> to me…

As I was coming to this realization for myself, it dawned on me. If I would rather have my son at home engaging in a learning activity and in a safe space, then it was my responsibility to regulate that space and *engage* in my child's learning activities. This was one way to preserve a true *relationship* with my child in a healthy way. Even if you prefer that your child play outside the way you probably did as a kid, it is still vital to be involved in your child's learning style and influences whenever you have the chance. We learned the importance of this on level one and can expand on it here in level two. The *cheat code* here is to *pause*, and truly *overstand* your role.

Never trust anyone or anything else to fully educate your children. Always be willing to be involved as a parent or guardian. It may be easier or require less work to have your children to learn elsewhere. However, the lessons they learn or do not learn could hurt them in the long run. It is imperative that you put in time and effort with your child. Learn with them and don't solely rely on the education systems, political systems, television, or everyone else to educate your child. Stand up and be sure to be an active educator in your child's life. If you are uncertain, be sure to do the research yourself. It is perfectly ok to reach out to others. Talk with those who work with children and understand gaming if you need guidance or need more resources. No one has completely figured this out, I sure didn't! This book was written as an intentional conversation partner. So, if you don't have a person in mind, you can still work through this guide. There is room for great progress if you really dig deep, open up, and engage!

Bonus: You and your gamer can learn together; learning together can increase your relationship bonding. So, engage in those **Duo-Discovery Moments**. They are quite fun!

With evolution comes new theories, case studies, quantitative and qualitative data, and new experiences. We tend to lack the ability to transition into *current* times and the newer societal norms. With each new decade we experience change. Heck, technology seems to evolve every 6 months, even though it feels like it evolves every 3 months or sooner! I swear it was yesterday when I was playing the *Nintendo Wii* with my Sun and that was eons ago. (The *Nintendo Wii* is discontinued now). Another example of change and technology enhancements are our phone/device updates. I feel like my phone attempts to force updates once a week now. Things are evolving quickly. If we stay dedicated to old ways of thinking, what we've *always known,* or only what is *familiar* to us, it isn't going to help us transition effectively with our children. In fact, based on my observations, it pushes us farther away from one another.

Hearing my child yelling at his *game acquaintances*, forgetting to eat, staying on the game until the "wee hours" of the morning practically drove me crazy! The game and *YouTube* seemed so distracting to me. Often, this is how I was thinking before *overstanding* what was really happening. I felt as if my son wasn't learning or partaking in any worthwhile experiences while doing all this *online stuff*. Let's just say I was wrong. Here's what really happened, and what I discovered when I was willing to *pause* and *overstand* my role in this game of life.

After one moment of frustration on top of another moment of frustration and a great deal of prayer, I decided to dig into my textbooks, a few papers, and years of study. This digging led me to a mirror of myself. I was required to look within, become more self-aware, and find out what was next. I chose to get on my son's level; I became intentionally involved to see what I could discover from his point of view. Low and behold, I learned a lot *for myself* and realized that while he played these games, he was learning too!

The future of society is wrapped up in a device we call cellular phones. Children learn a great deal through this device, social media, *YouTube*, gaming etc. They are glued to their phones and are susceptible to anything and everything. (It is the same for us too if we are honest with ourselves).

This is why there is a sense of urgency placed on this relationship building experience. I find *teachable moments* while communicating with my son. Please note, these *teachable moments* are reciprocal. Sometimes they are for him, sometimes they are for me and oftentimes they are for both of us. I am not sure about you, but if it weren't for gaming during the COVID-19 shut down, my son would have had much less peer social interaction, if any at all. *Pausing* to address my thinking brought me back to when I was younger. Remember when you were a child and simply wanted someone to listen to you or be heard? Well, this book is going to encourage you, and hopefully help you *overstand* the importance of bonding with your child on their level. Like, eye to eye level... So, get ready, it may feel odd at first, but it will feel great in the *end game*. It is time for you to Stand Up!

FPS TIME!
(First Person Shooter, Time!)

Seeing through Your Gamer's Eyes & Interacting in Their world

Goal 2: To *pause*, and make sure you are approaching this game of life and the role *you play* in your gamer's life from an authentic and holistic place.

(*Remember, patience is key.* It is okay to press *pause*, while playing the game and in real life. Give yourself some grace, be kind to yourself. This goal may take a moment to process and execute).

Why is this important?

Until now, most of us have accepted this new gaming culture. When our children, scholars, family members, significant others and/or friends spend time on the game it is the new "normal." Unfortunately, we have intentionally or unintentionally decided to disengage from their gaming experience. Fortunately, we can decide to overcome this former way of thinking and choose to get involved as we seek to foster the relationships we adore.

We are not learning about our gamers and the games they play simply to gain mastery over the conversation. Instead, we are learning to create a bond with our gamer. This requires that we deal with any roadblocks we might have in our thinking due to the rapid changes in society including in technology.

Light-Bulb Questions: Ask yourself, "What is my relationship to gaming? How have I been involved in my Gamers gaming experience? Have I purchased any games for my child?" If so, "What was my desired outcome? What has frustrated me most about the game and my child's engagement with the game?" Is my frustration related to the time spent away from my child because of *gameplay*? Is it related to a change in behavior from my child? What core beliefs do I need to address to make room for my child's current experiences?"

Be open to your true instinctual answers. Have compassion for yourself. You are learning and growing too. Give yourself time to reflect on your responses fully without interrupting your own thoughts and write them down.

Bonus: Remember, you can use the journal section in Level 8; Your Story, Your Level to capture your thoughts. I will keep reminding you to do this for a little while, until it becomes a habit.

Cheat Code: *PAUSE & OVERSTAND YOUR ROLE*

When I made space for my son by self-reflecting first, I experienced my son's genuine excitement to share all that he knew about his game with me; even though some of it went way over my head, lol. He was also probably so happy that I wasn't feeling and speaking negatively regarding his intense *gameplay*. Instead, I wanted to be ***involved*** and ***overstand*** his experience.

What Light-Bulb Question(s) will you ask? (Feel free to come up with your own questions).

Date: _____   Time: _____
Place: _____

_____
_____
_____
_____
_____
_____
_____
_____
_____
_____
_____
_____
_____
_____
_____
_____
_____
_____
_____
_____
_____
_____
_____
_____
_____

How did your child respond? What communication took place? How do you feel?

Date: _____ Time: _____
Place: _____

_____
_____
_____
_____
_____
_____
_____
_____
_____
_____
_____
_____
_____
_____
_____
_____
_____
_____
_____
_____
_____
_____
_____
_____
_____
_____
_____
_____
_____
_____

I am so proud of you! You are taking the necessary steps to build your gaming relationship. Whether it went well in your opinion or not so well, what did you learn from this *teamwork* experience?

Date: _____   Time: _____
Place: _____

_____
_____
_____
_____
_____
_____
_____
_____
_____
_____
_____
_____
_____
_____
_____
_____
_____
_____
_____
_____
_____
_____
_____
_____
_____

Level 3: GAME Loading...

The History of Gaming and Overstanding the Game Ratings

THE HISTORY OF GAMING:

While drafting this book, I'd finally accepted this *gaming movement* as a part of my current and future life experiences. Now that this was apparent, I started to wonder about the history of gaming. Questions were invading my mind, and I wondered who pioneered this movement? Doing a deeper dive to comprehend the culture of gaming was important to me. In my findings, I discovered not one, but two key people! The first person is known as the *Father of the Game Console* and the next person is known as the *Father of the Video Game Cartridge*.

Bonus: This information may not assist as it pertains to your relationship with your gamer directly. However, indirectly, it can be an enjoyable conversation starter and will give you a little background just in case you are curious too.

According to Steve Mullis from the *All Tech Considered magazine*, "... it was a sultry summer day in 1966 when Baer — who was working as an engineer for defense contractor Sanders Associates, now part of BAE Systems — scribbled out a four-page description for "game box" that would allow people to play action, sports and other games on a television set. One Sanders executive saw potential in Baer's idea and gave him $2,500 and two engineers to work on the project. Over the years they churned out seven prototypes in a secret workshop, before landing on a version that Baer and Sanders would use to file the first video game patent in 1971. The "Brown Box" was licensed to Magnavox and went on sale as the Odyssey in 1972 — the world's first video game system. The primitive system was all hardware and used "program cards" for games. Plastic overlays for the television screen provided color. Priced at $100 (though Baer had recommended $19.95), the Odyssey sold more than 100,000 units its first year and 300,000 by 1975."

From "game box" to the world's first video game system. The history of this worldwide phenomenon was intriguing. This research led me to my next discovery, *The Father of the Video Game Cartridge, or the Father of Modern-Day Gaming* (this pioneer has been named as both). According to Mike Snider, "... there's an oft-forgotten person from that era whose contributions to the industry still resonate today: A Black Engineer named Jerry Lawson."

Snider continued, "Lawson oversaw the creation of the Channel F, the first video game console with interchangeable game cartridges – something the first Atari and Magnavox Odyssey systems did not use. Those initial consoles had a selection of games hardwired into the console itself. (The Magnavox Odyssey, released in 1972, also used game "cards," that were printed circuit boards, but did not contain game data as the subsequent cartridges did.)

But Lawson, an engineer and designer at Fairchild Camera and Instrument Corp., led a team at the Silicon Valley semiconductor maker charged with creating a game system using Fairchild's F8 microprocessor and storing games on cartridges."

During a speech at the 2005 Classic Gaming Expo in San Francisco, Lawson stated, "A lot of people in the industry swore that a microprocessor couldn't be used in video games, and I knew better." The Fairchild Video Entertainment System, *Channel F* (for "Fun"), which began selling in 1976, had games such as hockey, tennis, blackjack and a maze game that foreshadowed Pac-Man. *Channel F* was a groundbreaking device that allowed players to switch between different games without having to purchase a new console. Lawson also built his own coin-operated arcade game called "Demolition Derby" in his garage. He was extremely intelligent and known to be able to fix almost anything. His passion and expertise led him to a home inventors club called the Homebrew Computer Club. This club represented a group of computer enthusiasts that included *Apple* co-founders Steve Jobs and Steve Wozniak.

Bonus: Jerry Lawson was the only Black member of the Homebrew Computer Club and he was inducted into the International Video Game Hall of Fame in 2011. He was an early proponent of the idea that video games could be used for educational purposes.

When he left Fairchild, Lawson founded his own video game company, Video Soft, which created games for the Atari 2600 and made some of the first 3D games. But he closed the company during the *Video Game Crash* of 1983. *(WorldsFacts.com, 2023)*

Thinking about the history of gaming and the path to its global exposure is truly fascinating to me. There is so much more history, but I just wanted to give you a little background. Developmentally, technology and the game movements are massive. The game options available are vast and growing! So, what is the old saying? If you can't beat them, join them. Our journey is ALL about *Overstanding* and joining them! Therefore, we are going to continue to learn, so we can foster and edify our relationships with our Gamers. Next, you will learn more about **Game Ratings** as you dive deeper and continue to expand your knowledge of Gaming.

OVERSTANDING THE GAME RATINGS:

What did the *History of Gaming* have to do with *Game Ratings*? For today's gamers, it may be impossible to imagine that the now $100+ billion video game industry ever hit a sharp decline. As mentioned previously, in 1983, the bottom fell out of the video game business in a devastating way. This infamous crash saw revenues plummet by 97% in just two years. Companies went bankrupt and had to close their doors. The future of video gaming was in serious jeopardy.

The Development of the Ratings System is partially responsible for the 1985 comeback of the Video Games. The creation of a video game ratings system (e.g. E for Everyone, T for Teen) gave consumers clarity on which games were age appropriate for their children. This new rating system was a key factor in the rise of video gaming. It was a game changer (pun intended)!

"Today, nearly two-thirds of American homes have household members who play video games regularly. And it's really no wonder: Video games have been around for decades and span the gamut of platforms, from arcade systems, to home consoles, to handheld consoles and mobile devices. They're also often at the forefront of computer technology." (Mullen, 2022).

APPROPRIATE VS. INAPPROPRIATE:

In the gaming world there are ways to identify the age-appropriate level of each game. This is called the game rating. You will find this rating available on the cover or case of the game itself as well as somewhere during the uploading of the game before play. In my own research, I came across the *Entertainment Software Gaming Board*: "Ratings Guide," a non-for-profit, gaming industry resource page active since 1994, to help inform gamers and *especially* parents. I was fascinated and encouraged by the intentionality behind this online resource:

The ESRB rating system was founded by the video game industry in 1994 after consulting a wide range of child development and academic experts, analyzing other rating systems, and conducting nationwide research with parents. ESRB found that parents wanted a rating system that has both age-based categories and concise and impartial information regarding content. With this philosophy in mind, today the ESRB administers a three-part system that includes Rating Categories, Content Descriptors, and Interactive Elements. (Ratings, ESRB.org)

Content Descriptors are applied relative to the *rating category* assigned and are not intended to be a complete listing of content. When a *content descriptor* is preceded by the term "Mild" it is intended to convey low frequency, intensity, or severity. I have provided a common chart listing the various categories of *game ratings* as well as a list of *content descriptors*. This is for your personal resource and for monitoring what type of games your gamer might be engaging in. To help us grow in our ability to engage with gaming appropriateness conversations, I have also shared some ***IRL*** (In Real Life) moments between my son and I that fostered these conversations.

Ratings

E	The Game is for Everyone
E 10+	The game is for those 10 years +
T	The game is for those 13 years +
M	The game is for those 17+
A 18+	The game is for those who are 18+ (Adults Only)
RP	The Game is 'Rating Pending'
RP 17+	The Game is 'Rating Pending' with the likelihood of having a rating for those 17+

TABLE 1. ESRB RATINGS AGE RANGE + SYMBOL

These are the *content descriptors* you will find on this website:

Alcohol Reference
Blood
Comic Mischief
Drug Reference
Gambling Themes
Strong Language
Strong Sexual Content
Tobacco Reference
Use of Drugs
Violence
Animated Blood
Discolored &/or unrealistic depictions of Blood
Blood and Gore
Crude Humor
Fantasy Violence
Intense Violence

Language
Mature Humor
Partial Nudity
Sexual Content
Sexual Violence
Lyrics
Nudity
Real Gambling
Sexual Themes
Simulated Gambling
Strong Lyrics
Suggestive Themes
Use of Alcohol
Use of Tobacco
Violent References

With these ratings in mind, please be sure to monitor the types of games your child plays. Make sure you are taking the time to discuss the diverse types of activities that occur in these games. Even though our children mature in between the release dates of these games, it is still important to do your research on the games. Remain aware of the visuals, language, and the depictions being presented to your child. As you learn about the *things* that happen in the games, teach your children about the events surrounding them in real life. Create conversations about these activities and make sure they are playing games you feel are appropriate for them to play. It might be time for your child to *overstand* how the games can impact them on deeper levels.

In Real Life [IRL] 1:

"I am sorry Mom for the language you may hear or for some of the names of the other gamers. Some of their names are inappropriate, they are random people, and I can't control what they say or call themselves". I said, "Thank you for your apology and you don't use that language, right?" He said, "Right Mom." Now, I know for certain a word or two may slip out that he should not say. However, I am certainly appreciative of his manners and respect for me. I am hoping this respect will follow him all the days of his life and that he will continue to respect others. Knowing what is appropriate versus what is inappropriate is key and will help him on various levels in life. Especially as he continues to prepare for high school, college, and beyond.

As parents, guardians, school leaders, and even partners it is important to be extremely mindful of the games your child or gamer is playing, who they are playing with, and the types of conversations they are having. Be sure to check the game rating, observe gaming interactions, and monitor them closely. Some of the games have in-boxing or direct messaging capabilities. As much as we want to believe this is a safe world, unfortunately, there are some very unsafe situations that occur. Our job is to keep our gamers as safe as possible.

The conversations during practice and play modes can also be too mature for your child. Be sure to have *real* life conversations with your children about what is going on in the world, on age-appropriate levels. Make connections with them that they can internalize. Connections that are relatable for your child's age group can help them comprehend the impact of their experiences and worldview. If the topics discussed in story mode, the gamer conversation, or any other space surrounding communication and the game are inappropriate for you to discuss with your child on a personal level, then your child should not be allowed to play the game. I know it may be tough to think like this at first, but again... You are the trusted adult in the child's life with the responsibility to keep them safe and to regulate their

Health Points as a real-life gamer and human being. It is vital that you have input on this journey. Trust me, you do not want your child to learn from what they watch and see *only*. We must be ready, open, and willing to learn with and for our children.

In Real Life [IRL] 2:

"I have to shoot him first, and this gun isn't big enough... there are too many of them!"

Although guns and firepower aren't always the most comfortable topics to talk about, gamers are learning about both. They will learn how many rounds certain guns can hold, the power of the gun based on the damage it creates, and more. I am hoping my Son will *overstand* the severity of the harm that guns (and those with guns) can cause. I speak with him about the various realities surrounding guns. Remember, either you talk to your child and join the learning experience, or they will learn on their own. Either way they will learn.

Lawson stated, "Most of the games that are out now – I'm appalled by them," he told *Vintage Computing and Gaming*. "They're all scenario games considered with shooting somebody and killing somebody. To me, a game should be something like a skill you should develop – if you play this game, you walk away with something of value. That's what a game is to me." As he aged, Lawson became upset with how video games glorified violence. (Snider, 2020).

My son and I have talked about how a gunfight in a game may end in victory. However, the *presumed power* it gives characters is not the type of power one should want. I made sure he *overstood* that guns are unsafe when not utilized properly. He asked a few questions, and I answered. We continued to talk about guns, and society, and various things that are going on in our communities, our state, and our world. This conversation and aspect can be extremely sensitive, especially if you have individual experiences with guns, the impact of them, and beyond. In this case, I suggest you come up with your own questions to engage and facilitate the conversation. I will still provide a few questions for you to reflect on. However, it is just to help you as you begin to brainstorm on what works best for you and your child.

Bonus: Be sure to note which games have death included. Those with ratings that have Teen or Adult content may not be the game for your child depending on their age. Some of the content in these games can expose too much. Age appropriateness is profoundly serious. Sometimes your child is hunting another person, other times they are being hunted. Many times, they are striking and killing others or vice versa. It is critical to practice intentional engagement during these moments.

Take the time to communicate, be open to your gamer's questions. Try to engage without bias and do your best to be open to what you may encounter. Hopefully, this will inspire future family learning moments. What are some types of conversations you should be prepared to have? This is the part I was not ready for; I mean, I knew I would have to discuss it eventually, just not so soon. Nonetheless, I quickly adapted and engaged in conversations held around death, life, violence, protection, healing, etc. I had to *level up* and you can too. Welcome the communication and continue to be and operate in a *safe space* for your child. Be completely honest about how certain parts of this journey make you feel and let your child do the same.

The goal of **Intentional Engagement** is to be an active listener. A term that fosters effective communication by listening to hear and understand, rather than listening just to respond. The listener is taking the time to process what the speaker is saying, and they are both reaching to *overstand* one another. This effective communication style includes asking intentional questions to gain clarity before formulating a response to what one is hearing. When one is listening just to respond this means the listener isn't fully paying attention to the speaker because they are so focused on what they want to say. It can also mean that comprehension, or true *overstanding* and engagement are not occurring. This lack in communicating effectively can result in low empathy, intolerance, and a disconnect between each person in the conversation. You will encounter the following statement a few times in this guide, because time is extremely precious. The time we spend communicating should be as intentional as possible, especially with our loved ones and community members.

In Real Life [IRL] 3:

"Look at all these dead people." This was definitely a *different* game, and one that I didn't ask too many questions about because I don't like gruesome games or zombie games. Even though I don't engage in these kinds of games, I am aware that he plays a few. Speaking about death is tough for me, but it is a reality. I've recognized that some of these games can help to spark healthy conversations surrounding life and death. This is why it is so important to get engaged and stay engaged to build an ongoing healthy relationship with your child.

Life and death are very real things that occur in life. Just be sure you, or someone you trust, are the ones to help them process what is going on. Many times, I would just watch my son play games to see what type of scenery, settings and situations were being exposed. However, as I began to engage in the process of **Getting Above the Mis-Education**, I learned to get involved and eventually cultivate many conversations around the game's storylines and other content. If your child is playing an uncomfortable number of games portraying death and killing, try to ask if your child wants a new game to add variety to their play.

MONITORING THE RATINGS:

Within the game rating and labeling system there are also categories labeled, *interactive elements*. These elements are important to note because they offer a lot of virtual freedom concerning making purchases and sharing your information with other gamers and the virtual world. These elements include:

In-Game Purchases:

Contains in-game offers to purchase digital goods or premiums with real world currency, including but not limited to bonus levels, skins, music, virtual coins and other forms of in-game currency, subscriptions, season passes and upgrades (e.g., to disable ads).

In-Game Purchases (Includes Random Items):

Contains in-game offers to purchase digital goods or premiums with real world currency (or with virtual coins or other forms of in-game currency that can be purchased with real world currency) for which the player doesn't know prior to purchase the specific digital goods or premiums they will be receiving (e.g., loot boxes, item packs, mystery awards).

Users Interact:

Indicates possible exposure to unfiltered/uncensored user-generated content, including user-to-user communications and media sharing via social media and networks. *(Be mindful, your Gamer may have the ability to connect with people from all over the world).*

Shares Location:

Includes the ability to display the user's location to other users of the app.

Unrestricted Internet:

Provides unrestricted access to the internet (e.g., browser, search engine)

ERSB Monitoring: ERSB has an application (app) you can download, allowing you to search any game, any time, and receive a rating summary. The summary will give you details on the content and context of the game.

In Real Life [IRL]:

Did I hear someone say Modern Day Pen-Pal? You bet, once they are on the game, children can connect with anyone from around the world. When I say anywhere, I mean *any*where and E-VE-RY-WHERE!!! When I was growing up and while at school, we had to write letters to have pen pals. After writing our letter based on a little piece of information that was shared by our teacher, we put the letter in an envelope, placed a stamp on it, and sent it halfway across the world. Next, we waited in high anticipation with hopes for a response. Getting a letter back was a great feeling. Yet, it seemed to take forever if it happened at all.

Fast forward to current times, there is no wait. The only instance while gaming where there would be "wait time" is if the system is buffering, if WIFI is not working correctly, or if a game is updating. The response time now is almost immediate. The gaming experience provides an ***Instant Virtual Pen-Pal***. Today, it is easier for children to meet others from another city, state, and country. Again, be sure to monitor their accounts.

Here are some of my tips: Do they have a PS5? If so, have them register with your email account so you can get updates and emails regarding games they choose to add etc. Be sure to stop and check-in for a quick touch point with your child while they are on the game, sporadically. You will know you are one of the *cool parents* or observers when your child's friends speak to you through the gaming system's audio, because they know you have entered the room, LOL. I know because I have leveled up to being a *cool Mom*. They speak to me! Every now and then, keep a close ear to the conversations that occur to ensure the words, phrases, games, and conversations during play are acceptable. Keep in mind that some of these games and apps have private chat features, so be sure to look out for this and review these platforms often.

Make a habit of checking the parental warnings while looking these games up to see what others are saying about the games. Due to my son's age, there are certain games that are not acceptable in my book. Please be mindful as you research the games and check to see who your gamer is playing with. If they are his *friends or associates*, you can contact the parents or guardians and begin to build relationships. Some of these friends may be ones you already know. In conclusion, follow up, be present, check in, and stay engaged. This *intentional engagement* is like a teacher's presence that continuously walks around to monitor their class.

If the teacher sits at their desk all the time, it is more than likely the scholars will start to deviate from the rules of the class and try to get away with more. However, if a teacher is walking around, making their presence known, misbehaving is less likely. Encourage your child to get off the game and their phone *at least* an hour before going to bed. Their brain needs time to wind down and reduce stimulation. If your child has difficulty falling asleep after getting off the game, it could be because their brain is still racing and is highly active due to *gameplay* or phone time.

FPS TIME!
(First Person Shooter, Time!)

Seeing through Your Gamer's Eyes & Interacting in Their World

Goal 3: To involve yourself in your gamer's world of gaming. To continue to learn more about your gamer and their experience while also identifying the *game ratings* attached to the games. The goal is to avoid games that are too mature, don't align with your values, or encourage harmful behaviors and mindsets. To engage in conversations with your gamer that discuss the actions, storyline and observed activity while encouraging age-appropriate *gameplay*.

Why is this important?

It is vital to monitor the types of games your child plays. Make sure you are taking the time to discuss the different types of activities that occur in these games. Historically, Jerry Lawson stated his concern regarding the glorified violence represented in video games. The more you *overstand* the game ratings, the better you will be at connecting with your gamer and creating safety in their gaming world. This level of involvement can also help you identify behaviors or behavior changes in your gamer. Overall, you want to be aware of your gamer's experiences to ensure they are mentally, socially, and emotionally astute.

Light-Bulb Questions: What do you know about the history of the creation of gaming systems? Do you know what happened in 1983? How does it make you feel to see people in the game lying down, not living? Have you connected some of these situations to real life? Consider discussing, "Although the game is simulated, the same guns that hurt people in the game can hurt people in real life." What do you know about guns, and is there a connection or correlation to the game your gamer is playing? How do the guns and actions in the game compare to guns and actions in real life?

Does your child have any questions? Is there some exploring you can do together pertaining to guns? How do you usually respond to inappropriate situations? How do you process them? Consider encouraging your gamer to share whenever they witness or hear something that makes them uncomfortable while playing the game and in real life. Let them know you will always be available to hear them out and need to know if they are ever uncomfortable to ensure their safety.

Bonus: Remember, you can use the journal section in Level 8; Your Story, Your Level to capture your thoughts. I will keep reminding you to do this for a little while, until it becomes a habit.

Assess, reflect, and create open communication concerning game appropriateness and your expectations. Lastly, if the game is too violent, gruesome, or if it is not age appropriate, please proceed with extreme caution, and suggest more appropriate games. Trust me, there are so many options of games to play available on various levels. Learning a language, playing sports, developing creative skills, participating in Game Shows, and many others are all possible in the world of gaming.

Cheat Code: *OVERSTAND THE HISTORY OF GAMING, THE GAME RATINGS AND* **G.A.M.E.** *(****G****etting* ***A****bove the* ***M****is-****E****ducation)*

What Light-Bulb Question(s) will you ask? (Feel free to come up with your own questions).

Date: _____ Time: _____
Place: _____

_____
_____
_____
_____
_____
_____
_____
_____
_____
_____
_____
_____
_____
_____
_____
_____
_____
_____
_____
_____
_____
_____
_____
_____
_____
_____
_____
_____

How did you or your gamer respond? What communication took place? How do you feel?

Date: _____ Time: _____
Place: _____

I am so proud of you! You are taking the necessary steps to build your gaming relationship. Whether it went well in your opinion or not so well, what did you learn from this *teamwork* experience?

Date: _____ Time: _____
Place: _____

_____
_____
_____
_____
_____
_____
_____
_____
_____
_____
_____
_____
_____
_____
_____
_____
_____
_____
_____
_____
_____
_____
_____
_____
_____
_____

Level 4: The Main Game

Overstanding the HP's *(Health Points)*

Balancing a Healthy Level of Gameplay

BALANCE:

To internalize the importance of balancing physical, in-person interactions and learning with virtual reality, we are going to discuss the health mechanic within *gameplay*. In gaming, the term "health" also known as "**Health Points**" or "**HP**" refers to the amount of damage a character can take before they are unconscious or killed, ending the game. Just as in my story with my son described in level two, anyone can start to deplete if they are moving too fast and not paying attention to their health levels. It was so fascinating and encouraging to see my son take pride in being the healer for his team, making sure they received the health they needed to get to the next level. Without health, a game cannot continue, this is the reason this section is also called *The Main GAME*. After pausing and taking a step back to *overstand* our role in our gamer's life, we can now be proactive about making sure our gamer *remains* in good health along their gaming and real-life journey.

Consider these few principles:

"For everything there is a season, and a time for every matter under heaven."

Ecclesiastes 3:1 (English Standard Version)

"There is a sufficiency in the world for man's need but not for man's greed." ~Gandhi

"All things are lawful for me," but not all things are helpful. "All things are lawful for me," but I will not be dominated by anything."

1 Corinthians 6:12 (English Standard Version)

We have the human agency to do what we please to an extent, however, everything should be done in moderation. This idea of living in moderation is not only in the bible, but both Plato and Aristotle wrote and published their ideas on the virtue of moderation. Their ideas had a significant impact on early modern England as argued in the book, The Rule of Moderation.

Anything good can become a bad thing if it is overdone. The time spent on the game isn't omitted from the principles listed above or *The Rule of Moderation.*

I want to *overstand* how gaming impacts my child's everyday life, while also making sure that my child grows into his best self. According to TechRepublic, an IT industry online database, user network, and research hub derived from parent company, Technology Advice, "The average gamer plays for eight hours and twenty-seven minutes each week." I know that my son's playing time exceeds this weekly average. Therefore, he needs to engage in educational material and in-person social interaction more often and one should not negate the other. He is still developing and growing mentally, emotionally, spiritually, physically etc. So, it is my responsibility to set clear expectations for my son.

In the article, "How to help Children Calm Down," by Caroline Miller, posted on ChildMindInstitute.org, setting clear expectations and routines provide structure which makes children feel in control. Clear expectations for behavior and *gameplay* can reduce and mitigate stress in children. It is ok to let your child know what the expectations are for their gaming experience. *Game ratings*, game time played, and behavior responses are key expectations that should be identified. This practice will also help to support future learning as it pertains to setting boundaries and self-discipline.

I have created strategies to help us monitor this experience. It can sound like saying, "Here's a healthy amount of *gameplay* I expect from my child, but I also expect a healthy number of other things such as: homework success, outside play, chore completion, and family time." We should not leave children with their own devices with no expectation of balancing their game time. One of the most effective strategies I use with *intentional conversation* and *engagement is the* "**Minute for Minute**" *theory.*

A gamer will spend hours and hours on the game, watching gamers, *YouTubers* and more. However, when it comes to things like cleaning their room, spending time with family, completing chores and even eating, it may seem cumbersome and irritating to them. So, when these issues arise, I simply ask my son to give the game a break. During this break these are some of the things we discuss and a few practices I created for us! We talk about time and how time flies when he is playing the game, but how reading a book for the same amount of time is something he considers to be *boring*. I then talk about how there must be balance. So, we pioneered the "**Minute for Minute**" theory.

In this "**Minute for Minute**" theory, my son must do something productive to build time in his **Game Bank**. For example, if he reads a book for sixty minutes, cleans his room for forty-five minutes, calls a family member for fifteen minutes, and helps me with a few of my educational or business tasks for thirty minutes, he has earned two hours and thirty minutes of play time. Now, he can play the game for the time he has earned. He can use it at one time or break up the time into separate gaming sessions. This strategy has been impactful. It helps him stay on a schedule and monitor his time accordingly regarding *gameplay*. This strategy has also helped my son process the true meaning of a minute; when he is playing, the concept of time feels different.

Another strategy we created together is "**Game Break Day**." Although we use the word *break*, these are days when he does not play the game at all. He takes a complete break from engaging with anything pertaining to games. "*Game Break Day*" may be necessary because he has gotten upset over the game; perhaps he is frustrated because he is not playing as well, or maybe it is just time to take a break. Acknowledging these moments are key to attaining real life Health Points to maintain a balance of *gameplay*. There are times that he also has taken ownership in his own frustration and conducted a **Ragequit** in the middle of playing. For all the reasons mentioned, "*Game Break Day*" is sometimes necessary.

Some resourceful activities that can be explored for, "*Game Break Day*," are the public libraries or parks in your area. Check out the events at the library and the park district of your neighborhood or cities and towns nearby. The Swan Libraries allow you to transfer your membership to all their branches. This means you can engage in activities and check out books at any Swan library, and they have a ton! Are there non-for-profits in your area that provide programs for kids? Whether it is for learning a new skill like swimming or language, or an instrument or acting; Consider what is around you that your child can take advantage of to balance their *gameplay* and human interaction.

This is also a suitable time to reach out to family members and friends to build connections. They need real experiences, in real time. We do not want our children to get too comfortable with virtual living to the point that they lack interpersonal and social skills all together. I've witnessed examples of this firsthand as a lead teacher who went from teaching online to transitioning back into the classroom. Scholars were not only behind educationally, but they were behind socially as well. School leaders and staff had to reteach social skills to foster healthy interactions in the school community. The gaming experience can have a multitude of impressions.

According to the TechRepublic article as previously discussed, a survey was conducted on the impacts of gaming and social development during the

COVID-19 pandemic. In 2021, 4,000 people were surveyed across eight countries concerning a shift in their gaming habits due to COVID-19. This survey gathered data stating that, "Fifty-three percent of respondents said they made new friends in a game and 36% ranked interacting with other players as an important component of a game".

As highlighted in Level One, "Overstanding Our ~~Child~~ **Gamer**, " has great depths. Finding a proper balance will be key and look different in each household. The context of social life has taken a major turn towards the virtual world, and virtual play is becoming a method for building genuine community. This survey was taken across eight countries, showing us, that gaming is also a worldwide phenomenon. This isn't just an activity that may be taking place in your household. This is an international experience many of us are having. In the twentieth volume of the Education and Health journal released in 2022, Mark Griffiths, a psychology professor from the U.K., shared research on the impacts of video game play on behavioral performance and learning.

> In their trial, Pope selected half a dozen 'Sony PlayStation' games and tested 22 girls and boys between the ages of 9 and 13 who had attention deficit disorder. Half the group got traditional biofeedback training, the other half played the modified video games. After 40 one-hour sessions, both groups showed substantial improvements in everyday brain-wave patterns as well as in tests of attention span, impulsiveness, and hyperactivity. Parents in both groups also reported that their children were doing better in school. The difference between the two groups was motivation. The video-game group showed fewer no-shows and no dropouts. (Griffiths, "The Educational Benefits of Videogames," (2022), 47-51.)

There is a great deal of education that takes place in *the game*. We should not place our personal belief patterns on our gamer when it comes to gaming simply because of our own frustrations, or lack of understanding of how it can help gamers in life. We should, however, seek to find the balance between our gamer's development in the virtual world and the in-person world. Watch children as they play the game and interact with other children in their neighborhood. To parents raised on a steady diet of movies and sitcoms, watching a child play Mario Bros for hours on end may not be particularly gratifying. However, that is the new point of reference. As they play, they solve problems, and often overcome instructions that are intentionally inadequate. This forces them to practice critical thinking. Gamers exchange playing strategies, memorize routes and create maps. They work long and hard to attain the gratification of finally winning a game. Professor Griffith's research also acknowledges that most of the negative consequences (of gaming) come from obsessive periods of game time. He shared that it is much less common to have negative symptoms of gaming when game time is balanced.

Keeping in mind the positive and negative effects of gaming and how we can help manage a healthy balance of game time reminds me of this saying, "The mind is a terrible thing to waste" versus "It's terrible to waste your mind." Words have power. We must be mindful of our thoughts and statements. A mind isn't terrible *ever,* this is why I prefer the second quote. We must be intentional with our thinking and our verbiage, while teaching our young ones the same. This is why I used the creative title of *Overstanding the G.A.M.E.* instead of Understanding the G.A.M.E. As I transitioned into this *Overstanding* process, I realized my Sun was certainly a Gamer, but I took it a step further. Being a gamer is not a syndrome or poor condition, or at least it does not have to be! He was so much more than that identifier alone. After internalizing this fact, I made changes. I focused on holding myself accountable, which eventually assisted in our personal growth and development.

Getting Above the Mis-Education (G.A.M.E.) requires that we go on our own personal journey of unpacking what we *think* about the game and its impact on our gamers. When we do this, we become *First Person Shooters* (FPS), opening our eyes and lenses to see what our gamers see, *overstanding* their experience in both the virtual world and the in-person world. Once we have done this, we can *choose* to learn strategies to help balance and navigate the development of our gamers. We can become healers in their lives, just like in the game OVERWATCH, mitigating the damage they take on through our awareness. Adhering to our gamers and supporting them *where they are* is essential in building and maintaining trust, as well as overall health in this relationship. It is time to lean in. Let's seek to gain Health Points virtually and in person! Continue to reach towards your Level Up and your Win!

Gaining Health Points [HP] 1:

"Mom, I won... I am number one and I started at one hundred!" This was *Fortnite*, a game that at one time seemed like the only game on the planet. EVERYONE was talking about and playing *Fortnite*. Various *Skins*, dancing, music, and reloading are the various things I recall most about this game. I remember thinking about how often my Sun had to reload, it was a lot. Making sure he had enough ammunition was particularly important. While observing, I learned that you don't want to run out of ammunition or run low on health. When you run out of ammunition, you can't defend yourself or your team, and when your health is low, you don't have the energy to proceed and reach your goal. Paying attention to your health is important. Being knowledgeable about when to reload in the game AND in life is a powerful tool. Timing is key in both scenarios.

Knowing when to pause to regroup, recalibrate, and reload are key factors of survival. If you don't reload you can't protect yourself. If you don't regroup you won't have the necessary nourishment to *keep going*. Navigating this experience will take practice. Setting your eyes on the goal and continuing to strive for it will be necessary. Learning how to find strategies while playing with other gamers (who may not be agreeable), is also something your child may experience. I have watched him play a game and get killed in the first minute. I have also seen him rank 100th (last) and fight each contender to become number one and win the game.

The moral of this section; Always press towards your goal no matter what or who is trying to stand in your way. I remember hearing a saying, "Fall 7 times, Stand UP 8!" One of my favorite motivational speakers, *Mr. Les Brown* says if you fall, fall on your back so you always have something to look up to! I am paraphrasing… but what I am pressing upon you and your gamer is to be victorious in your thinking! Look Up and Level UP!

Bonus: The Team Affirmations in Level Seven will help you with victorious thinking!

It is important to celebrate personal wins; I love how excited he was about his own progress. He was truly elated, and I was happy for him. Other people can want positive outcomes for us in our lives. However, if we don't believe in and acknowledge these things for ourselves, they may not happen. Encouraging ourselves and giving ourselves the grace we give others is also key in reaching for victories. Lastly, we must recognize that what is labeled as a victory to one may not be the same for all. This entire gaming experience is not a *one size fits all* type of experience. Everyone is different and I want all of us to embrace our uniqueness. It is the self-love and belief in oneself that will catapult you to the next level. I once heard a wise person say, "Sometimes the Victory is in your ability to last." So, start setting those expectations of balance, moderation, structure, and gaining Health Points with your gamer, while you still can.

Bonus: A win for them is also a win for you! It is also okay to take a couple of Losses (L's) because when you put them together, they form a W(in)!

My goal is to be my Sun's lifelong cheerleader and oftentimes model and coach too. With that being said, I must be cognizant of our Health Points and any imbalance due to the *overuse* of anything to cope with life. As parents, partners, or educational leaders, we must do our best to make the most of each moment with our gamer. If you've read my previous books, *Prayers for your Child from Head to Toe* or *Daddy's Girl*; "A True Love

Jones Story", you know that I speak of the importance of time. My quote states, "Time is something that is precious and so uniquely present that you cannot truly grasp it. You can't hold it or save it, but what you do within the time given is of importance." Tomorrow is not promised, and if I've learned anything during Covid-19 it's that each moment is precious. I am hoping this guide will help you acquire a more positive gaming relationship with your child and an *imprint* that will last forever.

FPS TIME!
(First Person Shooter, Time!)

Seeing through Your Gamer's Eyes & Interacting in Their World

Goal 4: To provide you with a convenient resource you can visit whenever you need to. To equip you with strategies to cultivate healthy experiences in your home between you and your gamer. These healthy experiences will help support the relationships you build with your gamer, his gamer friends, the community and beyond.

Why is this important?

When we seek to overstand the importance of balance and moderation, we can equip our gamers and children to become well rounded humans. Humans that will overstand that many of these lessons will extend beyond the world of gaming. These lessons will permeate into their lives and help them as they mature while making decisions that will impact their lives and others around them.

Light-Bulb Questions: The next time your gamer is playing the game, assess, "How many hours at a time does my gamer play the game? Does my gamer engage in the same number of in-person interactions as virtual ones? What areas of my gamer's schedule can use more balance? What healthy substitutions for gaming are available to my community? Am I being a good example of how to engage and disengage from my devices? How often do I stare at my phone? Do I model the balance and discipline strategies that I expect of my gamer? How can I partner with my gamer and support them both virtually and while engaging with others in person?"

Assess, reflect, and create some S.M.A.R.T. Goals. Habits do not change overnight. Allow your gamer time to adapt, and stick to the plan, they will get there! Well, you all will get there together!

Cheat Code: *BALANCE+MODERATION = HEALTH POINTS!*

What lightbulb question(s) will you ask? (Feel free to come up with your own questions).

Date: _____ Time: _____
Place: _____

_____
_____
_____
_____
_____
_____
_____
_____
_____
_____
_____
_____
_____
_____
_____
_____
_____
_____
_____
_____
_____
_____
_____
_____
_____
_____

How did you or your gamer respond? What communication took place? How do you feel?

Date: _____ Time: _____
Place: _____

_____
_____
_____
_____
_____
_____
_____
_____
_____
_____
_____
_____
_____
_____
_____
_____
_____
_____
_____
_____
_____
_____
_____
_____
_____
_____
_____
_____
_____
_____

I am so proud of you! You are taking the necessary steps to build your gaming relationship. Whether it went well in your opinion or not so well, what did you learn from this *teamwork* experience?

Date: _____ Time: _____
Place: _____

_____
_____
_____
_____
_____
_____
_____
_____
_____
_____
_____
_____
_____
_____
_____
_____
_____
_____
_____
_____
_____
_____
_____
_____
_____
_____
_____

Part 2

"Git Gud"! ("Get Good")!

Buff Your Gamer to the Next Level

Social-Emotional Learning Focus: 4 Sections

- ***SEL Focus 1:***
  SELF-AWARENESS
  IDENTITY, PATIENCE and PURPOSE

- ***SEL Focus 2:***
  SELF-MANAGEMENT
  FEARLESSNESS, CONFIDENCE & EMOTIONAL PROCESSING

- ***SEL Focus 3 & SEL Focus 4:***
  SOCIAL AWARENESS AND RELATIONSHIP SKILLS
  OBSERVATION, COMMUNICATION, & TEAMWORK

- ***SEL Focus 5:***
  RESPONSIBLE DECISION-MAKING
  SCANNING, PROCESSING, & OPPORTUNITIES

Level 5: Overstanding the XP's

G.A.M.E. MODE: SEL

<u>Helping Your Child Gain the Experience Points in Life to Ensure They Make it to the Next Level</u>

In gaming, there is something called an "Experience Point" or "XP". Experience points must be gained during play to get to the next level. No matter how many kills you get or races you finish you could remain on the same level if you do not collect enough points. In every area of life there are standards that determine if an accomplishment has actually been completed. Whether it is receiving a course credit, working for a specific number of hours, or attending a training and gaining a certificate. These standards are a lot like the experience points gamers must receive to advance. The U.S. Department of Education defines within the No Child Left Behind Act, that academic standards are set goals for what students should know and be able to do while learning academic content.

Standards help determine developmentally, grade-appropriate goals for students and teachers to work toward. Social-emotional learning (SEL) standards provide a "continuum of development across five SEL competencies: Self-Awareness, Self-Management, Social Awareness, Relationship Skills, and Responsible Decision-Making," according to the

Ohio Department of Education's K-12 Social and Emotional Learning Standards, 2019. Lessons surrounding Cognitive Development, *Soft Skills*, Life Skills, Critical Thinking, Social Emotional Skills, and Character Building are included in these *SEL* learning standards. I am a firm advocate of *supporting scholars* and meeting them where they need to be met. Making sure our gamers are getting as many experience points in life as they are in gaming is just one way to meet them where they are. We must have standards for our gamers in real time, just as we discussed in the last chapter. I believe that gaining an *overstanding* of the SEL standards and how to better equip our gamers with them will help us all get to the next level. This in turn will create healthier experiences within our households and communities.

Before we begin breaking down each learning standard and the many ways they can show up in gaming, I want to share a few resources that helped aid my understanding, research, and experience in the school system. One of those resources is the Massachusetts Department of Elementary and Secondary Education Learning Standards website. This website has a helpful circular diagram which breaks down these standards and includes examples. The Illinois Department of Education also has a website and downloadable document that breaks down each standard by grade level. (I've utilized these infinite times during my career). These resources can be found more in depth in the appendix section of this book under, "Social Emotional Learning" and are available in both English and Spanish. The SEL's we will be discussing were developed by an organization called *CASEL*, which is headquartered in the Chicagoland area. This organization was started by researchers, academic leaders, child advocates, and educators alike who were passionate about the future of our school system and children's learning abilities.

The *CASEL* learning framework is centered around, "five core social and emotional competencies—broad, interrelated areas that support learning and development." Surrounding these five core competencies are the different environments where this type of learning takes place, and it includes classrooms, schools, family & caregivers, as well as communities. The Social and Emotional Competencies as defined by CASEL are:

Self-Awareness,
Self-Management,
Social Awareness, *Relationship Skills*, and
Responsible Decision-Making.

(Take a deep breath, you are doing great)! I will assist in helping you filter through these competencies as you learn more about helpful characteristics that can be enhanced through gaming. Throughout the next pages, you will fill your toolkit with "Keys" that will help you open the door to access your WIN with your gamer. Prepare to continue on your individualized path towards LEVELING UP!

Since gaining experience points requires active participation, the next few sections will be full of examples, dialogues, and action steps all labeled "Gaining the XP's." So, keep a look out for those to get a snapshot of what leveling up can look like!

Social-Emotional Learning Focus 1:

SELF-AWARENESS

🔑 KEYS: IDENTITY, PATIENCE, AND PURPOSE

The first Social-Emotional Learning standard (SEL) we are going to gain experience points in is **Self-Awareness**. The core competency of self-awareness is to understand our own emotions, values, and thoughts and to recognize how they impact and influence our behavior in more than one context. Developing a sense of confidence and purpose in the world is a key characteristic of self-awareness. This also means that you are aware of your strengths and weaknesses. In other words, one of the first areas of social emotional competency is to know who you are! The journey of Identity is such a vital part of life, we cannot get away from it. Identity directs the flow of our lives; this type of experience point we are going to gain together will help us level up in knowledge of gaming and in life!

Bonus: This is a wonderful opportunity for you and your gamer. Take it to heart and do the work. You will be glad you did!

Gaining Experience Points [XP's] 1:

One day while describing another aspect of the game my son shared, "I can switch characters, skills, clothes, and ammunition when needed depending on what my immediate goal is. My original attributes within the game can be changed to reach a goal." Most games have a customizing feature or profile. During the customization, the gamer may get to decide who they want to be, choose their look, or pre-determine what skills and tools they begin the game with. Ultimately, creating his character's identity.

In real life, we don't get to choose the hand we are dealt when coming into the world. However, we do have the responsibility of knowing where we are and where we have come from. From there, we can make conscious decisions about what we want in life and who we want to be. My son can determine what original attributes of his gaming character to change based on the goal he wants to achieve within the game. He must take an inventory first of what his character has, and then based on his goal, determine what he would like to change. Your gamer will learn to make mature decisions while having fun and becoming more self-aware.

Asking ourselves, what do we have access to? How quickly do I need to make this decision? What do I have in my hands? These types of questions aid this *self-awareness* process in a progressive and growth-oriented direction. Eventually, we will get into the learning competency of decision making, however, in real life we cannot make wise decisions for ourselves without being aware of ourselves. When we are aware of what's true about ourselves, we can manage and eventually assess well to make game winning moves!

In addition to identity and purpose, there is another characteristic of the *self-awareness* journey that we must consider. It is patience. It takes time to understand oneself. Just think about it, how long did it take you to fully understand the thoughts, feelings, and values that shaped you? Are you still learning? Probably. These things take time, and we cannot expect our young gamers especially, to get it right away. However, we can cheerlead them on and be helpful participants on their journey.

If you feel like you are having difficulty internalizing who you are, I would love for you to take some time to soul search and assess a little. It will better equip you to come alongside your gamer no matter what your ages may be. Try sitting still and looking in the mirror. Now, think about your identity. Who do you show up as? How would you like to show up? What are your expectations and desires? Are you moving in the direction you would like to go in life? Are you teachable? Is change on the horizon? Are you the example you are asking your gamer to be?

(Note: If this section is a bit *heavy* or if you have this feeling at any point while reading this book, please refer to Level 7: GAME MODE - AFFIRM and give yourself a BOOST! Be kind to yourself, take your time and be patient with yourself too).

Do you need a refresher on the reality of patience? Okay, we are going to switch games for a second. Only because it was after learning about this game that I realized *it* requires the utmost patience overall. Let me continue as I tell you about the *number one* game in the world. This game requires patience beyond patience. If you read the bible, it may resonate with you that this game might even take the patience of the Bible character *Job*. I will explain.

Gaining Experience Points [XP's] 2:

My son said, "Well *Minecraft* took me years to understand, it is basically a pixelated survival game but there are so many factors. You need different types of food, potions, block types, biomes, equipment, and armor. There are enemies involved, you have to find places to go and things to do to win." He also said this game is very meticulous and that it would take him twenty-four hours to explain everything to me. I was surprised at how much patience my son had to exude to learn, study, and play this game. Acquiring every piece of material and placing each piece strategically took time. The end goal is to build a home or some sort of structure.

In this game, the gamers are literally, virtual architects. When I asked my son how he would describe this game and what skills he thought were necessary to attain or gain while playing this game he said, "It's a lot Mom, but all in all it is an open world survival game that is unique, interesting, fun, calming and at times difficult". I love that he isn't afraid of levels and challenges! I think I could write a book on this portion alone, let's keep pressing though (I think you get the picture). Developing a healthy sense of *self* requires the patience to observe both internally and externally. The external work which leads more towards social awareness and relationship skills are so much easier to accomplish when one has already developed the rhythm of patience and observance of oneself. Hence, why the ability to be authentic and aware is pertinent in the overall social emotional competencies.

"Git Gud/Get Good!"
Buff Your Gamer to the Next Level

Goal 5: To take an inventory of the thoughts, values, and feelings that influence our behaviors and decisions, so we can become self-aware. While becoming self-aware, discovering one's identity, practicing patience, and pressing toward our purpose is how we will get to the next level.

Why is this important?

Having the ability to acknowledge and identify these **Keys** provide a solid foundation in acknowledging our feelings, managing emotion, and executing expression. When we *overstand* the importance of knowing who we are, we gain confidence about being who we are. Accepting and internalizing who we are is key to *self-awareness*.

Light-Bulb Questions: The next time your gamer is playing the game, assess, "How long does it usually take your gamer to learn a new game or level? Do they frequently change the attributes of their playing character to fit their goals in each level? Do they normally make the right decisions that allow them to win? How long does it take them to win?" Also consider a self-assessment, and ask yourself: "Where is my patience concerning my gamers amount of time on the game? Am I exuding patience when I'm observing them? Do I model patience in my interactions with my gamer while they are playing and when they are not? How often does my gamer exude patience on and off the game? Does my gamer play games that require them to practice patience? Do I have areas in life right now where I am longing for more instant gratification? If so, why is that?" Are there areas in my life that I can practice more patience?

Assess, reflect, and create some S.M.A.R.T. Goals. Habits do not change overnight. Allow yourself and your gamer time to adapt, and stick to the plan, you will get there! Stay the course!

Cheat Code: *IDENTITY + PATIENCE + PURPOSE = SELF-AWARENESS!*

What Light-Bulb Question(s) will you ask? (Feel free to come up with your own questions).

Date: _____   Time: _____
Place: _____

_____
_____
_____
_____
_____
_____
_____
_____
_____
_____
_____
_____
_____
_____
_____
_____
_____
_____
_____
_____
_____
_____
_____
_____
_____
_____
_____
_____

How did you or your gamer respond? What communication took place? How do you feel?

Date: _____ Time: _____
Place: _____

_____
_____
_____
_____
_____
_____
_____
_____
_____
_____
_____
_____
_____
_____
_____
_____
_____
_____
_____
_____
_____
_____
_____
_____
_____
_____
_____

I am so proud of you! You are taking the necessary steps to build your gaming relationship. Whether it went well in your opinion or not so well, what did you learn from this *teamwork* experience?

Date: _____ Time: _____
Place: _____

_____
_____
_____
_____
_____
_____
_____
_____
_____
_____
_____
_____
_____
_____
_____
_____
_____
_____
_____
_____
_____
_____
_____
_____
_____
_____
_____
_____
_____
_____

Social Emotional Learning Focus 2:

SELF-MANAGEMENT

⚷ KEYS: FEARLESSNESS, CONFIDENCE & EMOTIONAL PROCESSING

The next core competency from *CASEL* is called **Self-Management.** After gaining perspective on where our emotions, behaviors, thoughts, and values are coming from, we can now more effectively manage them. This core competency impacts the way we handle stress and navigate our internal risk and reward system, also known as our motivations. Our ability to meet and achieve the goals we have is a result of our *self-management*. On previous levels we've discussed our responsibility as the trusted adult to help our gamers balance their game time with other life activities. This balance creates discipline. In relation to the core competency of *self-management*, we want our gamers to get to a point in life where they can operate with moderation and discipline *on their own*. When we take the responsibility of cultivating balance by modeling it and creating expectations in our gamers' life, we set them up to Level UP and gain this competency in experience points (XP's) for life!

There are two characteristics in life that help us develop *self-management*. The two characteristics are fearlessness and confidence. Even though we discussed confidence a little before, we are going to dig much deeper here as it is even more actualized in *self-management*. When we are exposed to so many parts of our inner-self and the things influencing our thoughts, emotions, values, and behaviors, it can challenge us and make us uncomfortable. The process of self-awareness can be sobering and even unsettling at times. The person we are learning to accept when we look in the mirror does not always reflect our goals, does not always fit perfectly in the environment we are in, and sometimes does not always gel well with others. Taking the time to own who we are is detrimental. So, how do we navigate or manage who we really are? How does gaming bring out this core competency? Let's gain this experience point together.

Gaining Experience Points [XP's] 1:

"Mom, as you can see, we are under attack." I watched in awe, and they certainly were. However, this did not stop him from attempting to fight and accomplish his goals.

He was getting shot at and I was screaming at the television, "Stop shooting at him!" My son said, "I want them to shoot at me (and hopefully miss), so I know where it's coming from…" This was a bold statement. The power of truth. He was willing to take a hit, but at least he'd know what direction the negative energy and attack was coming from. Once he realized where the shots were coming from, he could develop a strategy and take cover. In life, just as in the game, sometimes he will have to be fearless. He will have to perform in the face of adversity. The odds may be against him and the negative energy may be present, but he will still need to put his best foot forward. He will need to be bold when learning and executing in his business, educational and relationship endeavors.

Yes, your child is also learning fearlessness while playing certain games! I assure you they are being brave and are learning to build upon their confidence. Confidence will take us further than we think, building our security levels to higher heights is an ultimate game changer! I have witnessed my son exude fearlessness and face opposition countless times. He is a superb actor and has stood in front of thousands of strangers to perform and act (as the main character). I noticed that *Main Character Energy* was one of the countless impressive classes and resources available at Dream Con this year. We are truly looking forward to learning and sharing more at Dream Con 2025.

I have watched my Sun fearlessly and confidently face situations throughout various times of his life. He is a hero in my eyes too. He was in middle school on a day we thought was a regular day, until it wasn't. The fear of a pandemic quickly began to sweep our nation. He was urgently sent home, we were all sent home… and *just like that,* life as we knew it was no longer the same. This was a brave situation to survive. For three years school wasn't the same, social life wasn't the same. Truth be told, *nothing* was the same; I can't even recall details of the last few years due to the **COVID-19 Blur**. All things suddenly came to a halt and my son embodied a powerful disposition through it all. He doesn't know that his strength made it easier for me during these times. The COVID-19 changes and lengthy period was a scary moment for us, even those of us with strong faith. His adaptability, protective disposition, and positive outlook was truly a *fearless* stance. Like I said, heroic.

The activities and actions we engage in eventually play out in our everyday lives. Facing new levels, opposition, and challengers were familiar to my son. My son was able to exude some of these fearless skills because he had been practicing them through his gaming experiences. In turn, it ended up helping me too! As responsible adults, we need to be aware of the positive influence attached to gaming. It is just as important to recognize when the influence isn't so positive. Once this is identified, we must encourage our gamers to participate in games that do!

Gaining Experience Points [XP's] 2:

"Mom, do you want to watch me play my game or play? My response, "I sure do, give me a second… Are we playing the one that I am going to win with my favorite character *Kitana*?" My son said, "No, I am going to win with my favorite characters and end it all with a finishing move." (Then, he laughs)… I give him a, "No You DIDN'T look…" However, deep down I loved his confidence!

Confidence, the more he practices playing games with his characters of choice, the more his confidence excels. He will get used to the move sequence, how to defend himself, and he'll learn his characters' strengths and weaknesses too. Learning to play with confidence makes a significant difference. Practicing and moving to new levels in the games will help to increase his confidence levels and the way he feels when getting on the game. Yes, I know... This is something that could seem so simple, but sometimes it is not.

Think about a time when you didn't feel confident regarding a task, project, relationship or internally (*self-awareness*), and once you gained that confidence how that felt in comparison. My goal is to remind my son of the importance of being *fearless* and *confident* throughout life. I want him to embrace the reality that he's got this! I want him to be encouraged, and I have the power to participate! This is an amazing feeling, and you can do the same no matter what level you are on with your gamer! My authenticity, enthusiasm, and willingness to engage creates space for building *confidence* for both of us. This space eventually leads to growth and healthy decision making for everyone.

My son learned how important it was to practice and how critical it was to have a positive mindset! Many times, *confidence* was the reason he won. He simply decided to win and carried that energy with him during gametime. I also enjoyed the confidence he shared when inviting me to play. This made me feel amazing and boosted my confidence as well! I was truly making strides and could feel all those negative thoughts and feelings disappear (especially when I played too). We called those Mom and Son **Gamedates**, and scheduled them sometimes!

I was now engaging with confidence, joy, and love. If I am honest, I was feeling better about myself overall. Prior to this realization, I was feeling like the game was more important than me. I lacked confidence in being able to relate to my son especially when it came to the game. I wasn't competing against the game, which is something I told myself (I call that a *story*). I am so glad that *story* and I were wrong. I was competing for my son's time and our relationship building opportunities. I have learned a great deal in my lifetime thus far and believe the theories, tips and information curated with my Sun have been the most impactful.

The confidence this experience has brought both of us is simply immeasurable. Considering this social emotional learning discussion, we must acknowledge another significant component in the *self-management process*. It is our emotions. We must acknowledge that it is perfectly okay for us to have emotions and to feel. Our responses to our emotions, how we treat ourselves and others in that space, is where we need to be mindful. Sometimes we can speak negative words to ourselves or others when we are stressed or upset. Most times, when faced with these emotions we choose one of three actions: fight, flight, or freeze. Soon after the disappointment happens, just before moving into an upset space is the moment that requires intervention. Sometimes the intervening moment is practicing deep breathing techniques, walking away from the game, taking a nap, getting a snack and nourishment, or participating in another hobby. Taking a break from the game is perfectly okay. The *Game Break Day* that was mentioned in level four may need to be implemented.

In addition, whenever my son would get frustrated from losing, I would remind him of all the times he *did* win and would ask him to search for and hold on to that feeling; especially the wins that came after a loss. Then, I would ask him to think critically and reflect on what he did differently in those tenacious moments. The answer is always: "I eventually won because I didn't give up, Mom."

Allowing your child to speak their truth and to practice finding solutions are healthy activities. If they don't answer your questions right away, it is okay to give them some time. *Productive Struggle* is a great exercise to use. It is pertinent to give children the time to process their thoughts and reach answers on their own. As much as I sometimes want to *fix* things for my Sun, I have learned that he will make mistakes and lessons will follow. Oftentimes, these mistakes make us better and have unforeseen, glorious outcomes. They make us more resilient, more observant, more aware, and more prepared. Heck, I made a mistake with my son prior to *Getting Above the Mis-Education,* and look what this mistake has turned into, an entire movement to help our world become a better place. We are leveling up one relationship at a time. I also know what it feels like to lose, and it isn't a great feeling. This is why I choose to empathize, meet my son where he is, and offer neutralizing practices to help him move forward in a positive manner. *Fearlessness* and *confidence* are all about perspective.

Bonus: If you are struggling with Confidence, I created a helpful tool for you! In Section 7: GAME MODE - AFFIRM of this resource guide, I have added a Team Affirmations Tool! This should help feed your relationship as you nourish it with positive practices. The positive thinking and consistency certainly altered the trajectory of our relationship. With practice and dedication, it will help and you and your gamer build your confidence levels too.

Gaining Experience Points [XP's] 3:

"Ugh, I lost. I am done playing for now." When he loses it really puts him in a place of frustration. I try to give him space during these moments. As mentioned earlier, I'd become his biggest cheerleader, I was really involved, it was really cool. Sometimes I'd try to engage and ask if he wanted to play a different game. This would give him the opportunity to step away from the game that was irritating him at that time. I also offered to play with him or watch him play the new game to add some fun and hopefully laughter.

Timing is everything. When he was open to it, I'd still engage in conversations that provided a positive perspective. I reminded him that he could always accomplish the *win* another time. It wasn't like he was playing at an arcade; he wasn't going to run out of "plays or turns". I also asked him what he did in the game that may have caused him to lose and what did he learn from that experience? It was important for me to explain the lessons that may come from *losing*. I told him that every time he plays, he can look forward to learning something new about his strategies. When looking to encourage your gamer, please don't ever say, "It's just a game". I made that mistake many times. It matters to them and just as you'd like grace when something matters to you, it is important to give that same grace in virtually curated spaces.

Being a *cheerleader* meant providing and participating in edifying conversations. I wanted him to look at the *silver lining* within each lesson and every lesson moving forward. My goal was to remind him to search for the lessons that accompany failure. We can usually *overstand* the lesson and become solutions oriented once we get through the initial emotion tied to disappointment.

Lastly, I choose to disclose times in my life where I've lost and learned. Please note, I am very transparent with my son. I am open about my mistakes on various levels. I tell him about firsthand experiences, business situations, heart matters and all in between. None of us are perfect; I'd rather my son learn from me and internalize that I am human too. Being his parent does not make me infallible. I want him to be prepared for the feelings, emotions, and thoughts that often come with disappointment. Many times, being transparent with my son allows us to navigate our emotions together, and it becomes what I like to call a "Duo Discovery Moment." How about gaining a few of these experience points for you and your gamer too? Let's reflect!

"Git Gud/Get Good!"
Buff Your Gamer to the Next Level

Goal 6: To gain the competency and ability to manage oneself when it comes to our emotions, thoughts, values, and behaviors from context to context. To take inventory of the hindering experiences that influence our behaviors, discover the lesson, practice confidence and press towards the next level.

Why is this important?

It is important for us to cultivate internal motivation to learn from our mishaps and to practice the power of positive thinking on our own. When we *overstand* the discipline of managing our emotions, we can better determine how we show up in the world and who we want to be. This will propel us towards fearless decision-making and winning moves in life!

Light-Bulb Questions: The next time your gamer is playing the game, assess, "How does my gamer react to losing the game vs. winning? How can I engage and encourage healthy processing of those emotions? What does it mean to be fearless to you? What is the best thing that can happen when you display fearlessness? What is the worst thing that can happen when you display fearlessness? Are you able to recuperate from whatever the worst thing is? Tell me about a time you lacked confidence. How does it feel when you have confidence about something? What is something you might experience in the future that may require confidence and why? Are you willing to schedule *Gamedates* with your gamer? If so, schedule one now if you are able!

Remember, many of these questions are helpful for you to answer as well. Get personal and reciprocate vulnerability in the conversation. Then, assess, reflect, and create some S.M.A.R.T. Goals. Habits do not change overnight. Allow your gamer time to adapt, and stick to the plan, we will get there!

> **Cheat Code:** *EMOTIONAL PROCESSING + FEARLESSNESS + CONFIDENCE = SELF-MANAGEMENT!*

What Light-Bulb Question(s) will you ask? (Feel free to come up with your own questions).

Date: _____ Time: _____
Place: _____

_____
_____
_____
_____
_____
_____
_____
_____
_____
_____
_____
_____
_____
_____
_____
_____
_____
_____
_____
_____
_____
_____
_____
_____
_____
_____
_____
_____
_____

How did you or your gamer respond? What communication took place? How do you feel?

Date: _____ Time: _____
Place: _____

_____
_____
_____
_____
_____
_____
_____
_____
_____
_____
_____
_____
_____
_____
_____
_____
_____
_____
_____
_____
_____
_____
_____
_____
_____
_____

I am so proud of you! You are taking the necessary steps to build your gaming relationship. Whether it went well in your opinion or not so well, what did you learn from this *teamwork* experience?

Date: _____ Time: _____
Place: _____

_____
_____
_____
_____
_____
_____
_____
_____
_____
_____
_____
_____
_____
_____
_____
_____
_____
_____
_____
_____
_____
_____
_____
_____
_____
_____
_____
_____
_____

Social Emotional Learning Focus 3 and 4:

SOCIAL AWARENESS AND RELATIONSHIP SKILLS

⚷ KEYS: OBSERVATION, COMMUNICATION, & TEAMWORK

The third and fourth core competencies are **Social Awareness and Relationship Skills**. We are going to process these two competencies in relation to one another because they showed up in similar ways as I observed my son's gaming. According to the *CASEL* model, *social awareness* involves recognizing how others think and being empathetic towards the experiences of others. There is an element of diversity and cross-cultural interaction that this core competency requires. In other words, we can't stay in our personal bubble and expect to develop this skill. When we are aware of and able to manage ourselves, it can make it easier to be aware of others, but we must be intentional about it. Otherwise, we might become self-absorbed and miss the gift of reality. This gift is harmony with and respect for others.

Like social awareness, relationship skills are related to how we navigate working with others, but let's take it a step further… When we become aware of someone else's needs, how do we respond? Are we actively listening and really hearing them or projecting our own thoughts on others? Do we offer empathy? Do we ignore them? Do we step into a leadership role and try to help? Are we team oriented, and do we own a collaborative mindset? These are helpful questions to assess how one navigates working with others. Some of the key characteristics that help us cultivate these two core competencies are *observation*, *communication*, and *teamwork*. How fitting, being that teamwork makes the dreamwork!

Gaining Experience Points [XP's] 1:

"Someone is alone and they shouldn't be." Wow, when he was walking me through his game and said this, my heart literally skipped a beat, and a smile covered my entire face. To be able to offer true concern in times such as these is a lesson that he and his friends can become familiar with. It is important to know how to identify when someone needs to be protected or cared for. It also means he's been observant and *overstands* when his teammate needs something.

"Jump in the robot for protection." When my son said this, it was clear that he knew his gamer friend needed protection. He also knew and could comprehend the urgency of this action and the potential outcome if he didn't jump into his robot for protection. The first level of power is to protect. We must be ready to take action when it is time to do so, starting with ourselves. How can this transcend into current moments of our life? How can we identify with this? This could be quiet time, personal time, prayer, meditation, and beyond. Seeking guidance and protection of the mind, heart, body, and soul are perfect starting points. Helping ourselves and acknowledging where we are can help us assist others in greater capacities. This moment was key, and it immediately took my mind to a quote of my own. "Sometimes we are in pieces, often ignoring the nudge and stillness of what our peace *says*." (S. Jones, 2024)

I promise the more I listen, engage, write, and type, the more I realize just how formidable gaming can be! It was during this observation that I realized my Sun needed *overstanding*, empathy, and concern *from* me as well. It was time for me to practice these characteristics too. My son was learning how to quickly assess coordinates and direction, engage in direct and goal-filled conversations, practice empathy and so much more.

 *Bonus:* Proudly speaking, I was too. If you stay the course, you will win as well.

In life, we all need someone sometimes, and it is helpful when someone pays enough attention to you to *overstand* when you truly need help. Physical help is one form of help to recognize, but mental and social emotional help is another form of assistance that isn't so easy to identify.

Being aware and paying attention to when you or someone else may be feeling alone, depressed, and in need of assistance could be a real-life game changer.

Being Seen is key and this is another reason it is important to be observant and self-aware. Sadly, suicide affects people of all ages. In 2021, suicide was among the top nine leading causes of death for people ages ten to sixty-four. Suicide was the second leading cause of death for people ages ten to fourteen and twenty to thirty-four. Recognizing the needs of someone else and for yourself are important. I have had a therapist a few times in life, and each time I have learned necessary information about myself, my story, and my overall truth. I have also been trusted to help with suicide prevention a few times. Talking to someone may save a person's life. I'm grateful that I was observant and able to assist during moments as tender as these. Being able to care yourself and others are important duties.

Gaining Experience Points [XP's] 2:

"Bro, you have got to stop charging into the battle Bro." He is solely focused on charging forward. He was communicating and learning to communicate clearly as he was guiding his teammate in this battle. He told him that he needed to assess the situation before charging in.

Isn't this also necessary in life? Shouldn't we, even as adults, learn to *assess the situation* prior to *charging in*? This is true for situations we experience as adults, up to and including how we choose to manage experiences pertaining to our children. Why not start with managing this *G.A.M.E.* situation differently? What if your communication and *overstanding* could be so much better? Would you be willing to put forth the effort to think and respond differently? These are the questions I had to sit with and ask myself. Was I really ready for change? I couldn't continue to do the same things and expect different outcomes. It was time, enough was enough. Change loading…

I simply got tired of yelling, "Get OFF the GAME, I am sick of hearing you argue! What are you learning ANYWAY? THE GAME just seems like a waste of time!" Ask yourself, is this type of communication helpful? Does it seem positive? Does it evoke *higher-level thinking*, a *safe space,* or a growth mindset for any of us? If I can be transparent, none of those expressions caused me to feel better. I actually felt worse as the wedge seemed to be growing between my son and I. Do you agree? Do you have similar feelings and experiences? I OVER get it (as my son would say), and trust me, you are in the right place. There is no time like the present and this moment is for you! You can do the work to create change. Trust me, I did it and you can too!

I am so grateful that as a *mama bear,* I finally took a moment to stop charging into battle and took time to *overstand* the situation first. This effort has opened our lines of communication and has forever altered our lives. I *overstand* so much more as it relates to the game, his friends, and of course, my son. That monumental day in March of 2021, I looked at the bigger picture and found our silver lining. This silver lining was one we could connect on and build from. This was the preface for the communication breakthrough, and I hadn't even realized the power of that moment, yet.

Let's broaden the lens. A breakdown in communication has the power to cause wars, dissension, separation, break-ups, fights, tension, etc. How many times have you gotten *into it* with someone because you misinterpreted a text message, didn't receive a message, misread body language, were too nervous to be truthful or simply ignored someone's efforts to communicate with you? It is important to practice effective communication. Gamers communicate consistently during game time. Plans, goals, techniques, and strategies are discussed. Again, life lessons are showing up here and little seeds of knowledge are being planted!

Bonus: Building and maintaining positive relationships with others are central to recognizing the thoughts, feelings, and perspectives of others, including those different from one's *own. In addition, establishing positive peer, family, and work relationships requires skills in cooperating, communicating respectfully and constructively resolving conflicts with others.*

Gaining Experience Points [XP's] 3:

"I see you, go ahead and run. I am on the roof and will get anyone who comes for you. I have your back." This is just one of the many quotes I heard my son say while playing the game. This made me smile, it was an example of *teamwork*. Learning to listen to others, being there for others with hopes to find common ground or to accomplish goals is important. This display of teamwork was an example of my son and the other player building a foundation of trust.

Gamers have to depend on one another to survive. This idea is one that will be shared and experienced countless times in his life. As he transitions from adolescence to teenage years and well into adulthood, he will create moments that involve teamwork. School projects, teams/clubs, family experiences and career projects will provide opportunities for him to practice working with others. Please believe our children are practicing this much needed skill while playing the game.

Gaining Experience Points [XP's] 4:

"Some healers have stronger powers than others in this game." There are certainly levels to everything in life. One of the healers had a bigger and more powerful tool to use while healing others. Another had a more powerful gun too. Levels are pertinent in the gaming world overall. Gamers reach higher levels as they get better. There are levels within each game you choose to play. Most of the time the first set of levels identify the difficulty level the game is set on. These levels are usually set to easy, medium, or hard. Once the level of difficulty is selected each level that is conquered gradually gets more difficult. The levels that are within a G.A.M.E. are so vast.

Overall, the idea is to exude the necessary skills to successfully navigate while playing. It is remarkably interesting how *the game* can mimic life. I started to think about how *levels* impact us. Levels are represented in numerous ways throughout our lives, and it was awesome to learn that my son was learning about proper protocol.

Wow, this learning was really happening! How many times do we need to acknowledge others' social, individual, or cultural differences? We must learn to demonstrate respect for individuals from various social, cultural, and economic backgrounds. Experience at this level can lead to advocating! Advocating for the rights of others, oneself, and for the common good are levels that require dedication. This is a concept that is usually identified for children in their late High School years according to the *Illinois State Board of Education Standards*.

There isn't an "I" in team, I know you have heard that before. Yes, as individuals, we must bring our best and share our greatest selves. We must show kindness, embody, and exude integrity, dedication, and hard work. Even with our absolute best efforts we need a team, we need to demonstrate working with others, learning from others, growing with others, delegating, and how to take constructive criticism or feedback. These experiences are necessary to grow spiritually, physically, mentally and emotionally. If we think about all the key moments in our lives, rarely would we say we didn't need any assistance or that we were alone for our entire journey.

"Git Gud/Get Good!"
Buff Your Gamer to the Next Level

Goal 7: To engage in the ability to practice teamwork, communication, and empathy. To develop a competent level of *social awareness* and *relationships skills* that allow us to level up individually, in our relationships and in our community.

Why is this important?

Everyone needs a teammate or someone by their side at some point. It is important for us to attain social awareness and build our relationship skills capacity. When we can observe what's happening around us, communicate, and exude empathy for others, we are better equipped to handle life!

Light-Bulb Questions: The next time your gamer is playing the game, assess, "Is my gamer regularly communicating with other gamers or often playing alone? How well does my gamer play when playing alone versus on a team? When my gamer communicates what communication styles arise? How do I communicate with my gamer when they are playing the game? Am I practicing *overstanding*? How do I view teamwork and what role does my gamer usually take when on a team?" How am I exuding trust with my *game*r? Are my relationships and my behavior examples of these same *Keys* and *Cheat Codes* I desire for my *gamer*?

Assess, reflect, and create some S.M.A.R.T. Goals. Habits do not change overnight. Allow your gamer time to adapt, and stick to the plan, you both will get there!

Cheat Code: *OBSERVATION + COMMUNICATION + TEAMWORK = SOCIAL AWARENESS AND RELATIONSHIP SKILLS*

What Light-Bulb Questions will you ask? (Feel free to come up with your own questions).

Date: _____   Time: _____
Place: _____

_____
_____
_____
_____
_____
_____
_____
_____
_____
_____
_____
_____
_____
_____
_____
_____
_____
_____
_____
_____
_____
_____
_____
_____
_____
_____
_____
_____

How did you or your gamer respond? What communication took place? How do you feel?

Date: _____   Time: _____
Place: _____

_____
_____
_____
_____
_____
_____
_____
_____
_____
_____
_____
_____
_____
_____
_____
_____
_____
_____
_____
_____
_____
_____
_____

I am so proud of you! You are taking the necessary steps to build your gaming relationship. Whether it went well in your opinion or not so well, what did you learn from this *teamwork* experience?

Date: _____ Time: _____
Place: _____

_____
_____
_____
_____
_____
_____
_____
_____
_____
_____
_____
_____
_____
_____
_____
_____
_____
_____
_____
_____
_____
_____
_____
_____
_____
_____
_____

Social Emotional Learning Focus 5:

RESPONSIBLE DECISION-MAKING

⚷ KEYS: SCANNING, PROCESSING, & OPPORTUNITIES

The fifth and final core competency we will discuss is **Responsible Decision-Making.** This core competency comes off a little more data driven than the others. This competency involves being able to recognize the risks and rewards of certain behaviors across social norms, while also making decisions for the well-being of oneself and others. It is one thing to recognize a need and choice that must be made. It is another thing to make that same choice with others in mind knowing the risks. Having the confidence to make decisions, utilizing social science skills represents a level of intelligence. This level of intelligence is a culmination and result of the other four SEL Skills. Three helpful ways to level up towards this fifth core competency are *scanning*, *processing*, and recognizing *opportunities*.

Gaining Experience Points [XP's] 1:

"I see how many rounds I have, the types of guns, other gamers' info, etc. I can see more than one view and there's lots of data on the screens to help us figure out what we should do." My son was able to use the information on his screen to help himself and his team survive another level. Whew! I was impressed and slightly overwhelmed by all of the information that was displayed at one time. I was even more impressed that he knew what every number, icon, or gauge meant.

As reported in a Caravel Research Journal Article written by David Corso and published through the University of South Carolina's online research database, video games are excellent pedagogical tools.

> Video games can provide immediate feedback, motivate players, set specific goals, promote mastery, encourage distributed learning,

teach for transfer, adapt themselves to the level of the learner, and provide various other teaching techniques. Whether it's promoting long-term learning through distributed practice or increasing a player's mastery of educational content, various elements of game-based learning intrinsically provide challenges that develop their students (Boyan & Sherry, 2011; Gentile et al., 2011).

Although it was information overload for me, I started to think of the benefits of having skill sets like the ones listed in the report. This *scanning* and *processing* ability could be helpful in various areas of my Sun's life. It may help him as he analyzes and problem solves for school related work. It may also help him socially and professionally. Being able to scan and quickly assess situations is a great characteristic to embody. As I continued to think of the many possibilities to expand this skill, I realized this would be helpful as he acquires his driver's license. When he learns to drive, he will be able to observe the street signs, the directions and what's occurring on the roads quickly. In conclusion, scanning, processing, and recognizing opportunities can be beneficial in various ways.

Gaining Experience Points [XP's] 2:

"Ugh... Darn I am running out of energy; I need to eat so I can make it to the next board." The quick processing of situations is pertinent, so gamers know how to maneuver. I can't begin to say how important it is to process information and to execute properly. This is going to help him overall from business to the most personal situations. Once you know the information, options, and the reality of anything, you can usually execute properly regarding *everything*.

Moving forward, he will begin to recall or memorize some parts of the game. He will most likely utilize this skill and learn lessons regarding processing. As he processes what will happen next, I'm hoping he will execute with the prior knowledge he's received. Isn't this what we do in life also? We evaluate our own moments, do the best we can, and have faith that

ALL things will work together for our good. Well, at this point in the game, this is all our children can do as well.

For example, if he is in school and knows exactly what he needs to do to attain an 'A', he can execute that plan if he chooses to work diligently. If he doesn't *overstand* something, he will need to go the extra mile to be sure he comprehends the concepts. Perhaps this could mean receiving tutoring, seeing the instructor after school, or finding other resources that may assist him.

Gaining Experience Points [XP's] 3:

"Darn it, I am looking for one specific tool and it is not here. I thought I had it." When he runs into issues in the game, it is pretty cool and interesting watching him work through those situations. Most times he takes the time to re-do what he's done, then he'll go the extra lengths it takes to solve the issue. The, "let me figure it out" attitude is going to help him a great deal in life. Instead of looking at everything as a severe problem, he can put on the lens of, "let's figure it out". He can ask himself, "What is my area of opportunity?" This type of mindset will certainly help him as he matures in life.

I would like to call these *areas of opportunity,* instead of problems. These are areas that offer us the opportunity to find ways around things we once called *problems*. I say, it is the gateway to what us educators call, "Productive Struggle." This place is helpful in life and provides room for growth. Productive Struggle is basically time allotted for a child or person to press through their critical thinking strategies as they develop answers to questions and find solutions. In the gaming world, I am calling it the **Productive Struggle of Gaming**. In that particular place, we have to allow the gamer time to figure it out! Give them the opportunity and space to discover an answer on their own. This answer may not be 100 percent correct. However, critical thinking, current experience and prior knowledge will help build their confidence and is a bright spot to look forward to.

We usually internalize and appreciate experiences that we have to work through. Oftentimes the frustrations we hear our gamers expressing are connected to their *Productive Struggle of Gaming.* Being solutions oriented is key here. Your gamer can utilize prior knowledge and their growing ability to scan and process their boards to determine their best course of action. Learning and growing will give them the space to be more successful as they gain more experience. These same tools and characteristics will be helpful as young gamers mature into adults and as adult gamers mature as adults. Spending time in the wrong spaces and in the wrong opportunities are also costly lessons that prevent us from progressing. Being able to recognize and discern the proper opportunities for one's life is essential. The ability to process issues at hand and move toward the best possible outcome is one lesson that will last a lifetime.

"Git Gud/Get Good!"
Buff Your Gamer to the Next Level

Goal 8: To equip gamers with strategies to make responsible decisions that will have an impact on their lives, their family's lives and those to which they are connected. Having confidence and the ability to scan and process information is key. This is key because the overarching goal is to create and seize successful opportunities.

Why is this important?

When we *overstand* the importance of scanning, processing, and recognizing opportunities we can become solutions oriented. This is a timeless life-long skill that is transferable to every field and level in life. Once you know the information, options, and the reality of anything, you can usually execute properly regarding *everything*.

Light-Bulb Questions: The next time your gamer is playing the game, assess, "How quickly are they able to make decisions in the game? Does your gamer ever think about the decisions they've made after they've made them while playing? What must happen in order for them to make a decision? Does it ever get confusing to look at the screen? What are the most important pieces of information that are available to them and to you? Is it okay to take time to think things through? How can you use prior knowledge to help you when you are playing a particular game? What do you think of when you hear the words *Productive Struggle*? Have you ever witnessed someone struggling to get to an answer? If so, what did that look like? If not, what do you think it looks like?"

Assess, reflect, and create some S.M.A.R.T. Goals. You are doing so well. Allow your gamer time to adapt, and stick to the plan, you all will get there! (Have you been using your Notes and Reflections section)?

Cheat Code: *SCANNING + PROCESSING + OPPORTUNITIES = RESPONSIBLE DECISION-MAKING!*

What Light-Bulb question(s) will you ask? (Feel free to come up with your own questions).

Date: _____ Time: _____
Place: _____

_____
_____
_____
_____
_____
_____
_____
_____
_____
_____
_____
_____
_____
_____
_____
_____
_____
_____
_____
_____
_____
_____
_____
_____
_____

How did you or your gamer respond? What communication took place? How do you feel?

Date: _____ Time: _____
Place: _____

_____
_____
_____
_____
_____
_____
_____
_____
_____
_____
_____
_____
_____
_____
_____
_____
_____
_____
_____
_____
_____
_____
_____
_____
_____
_____
_____
_____

I am so proud of you! You are taking the necessary steps to build your gaming relationship. Whether it went well in your opinion or not so well, what did you learn from this *teamwork* experience?

Date: _____ Time: _____
Place: _____

_____
_____
_____
_____
_____
_____
_____
_____
_____
_____
_____
_____
_____
_____
_____
_____
_____
_____
_____
_____
_____
_____
_____
_____
_____
_____

Level 6: G.A.M.E. Mode ·Skill-Check

Take the Pre-Quiz!

PRE-QUIZ:

I want you to take this quiz and answer each question honestly. This is a safe-space and judgment-free zone. Your authenticity will be helpful as you assess where you are now versus when you take the post-quiz at the end of this guide. I am hoping this interactive guide and your real-life application (of the suggestions within these pages) have an impact on your **Post-G.A.M.E. Score.**

Answer these questions on a scale of 0-10 (0 being "I Highly Disagree" and 10 being "I Highly Agree")

1. I am familiar with the ESRB rating system. _____
2. I know the names of at least three video games my child plays currently._____
3. I play video games with my child _____
4. I know the names of at least two other people my gamer plays video games with _____
5. There are benefits to playing the game _____

6. I can name at least five benefits or positive characteristics my child can attain from playing the game_____
7. My child and I have a great *overstanding* as it relates to their gaming activity _____
8. I engage in conversations with my child surrounding the game that help me *overstand* details pertaining to their experience. _____
9. I feel positive and at ease when my child plays the game _____
10. I am comfortable with the amount of time my child spends playing the game_____

Total Pre-G.A.M.E. Score: _____

Your score can range from 0-100 here is the breakdown of your score:

90-100 - You are doing a superb job and have a great 'gaming relationship' with your child! You certainly are at the LEVEL UP stage! You also have a phenomenal overstanding of your child, yourself and this new gaming world we are in. Be sure to continue to grow with your child and still complete frequent check-ins, have deep conversations and engage! Continue reading for more insight and be sure to purchase this guide and spread the word please.

80-89 - You are doing well and have built a solid foundation regarding the overstanding of your child and this new gaming world we are in. You are absolutely doing the work. Continue to press and engage in interactions with your child surrounding the game. Be sure to ask them questions, see if they can teach you how to play a few games. Create a safe space, carve out time to dive deeper. Practice identifying ways to combine the experiences and make them relatable. Keep up the magnificent work!

70-79 - You communicate with your child more than most. However, you could certainly build a better relationship with your child as it pertains to the game. There are great experiences waiting for you and your child. Continue reading for more insight. Your 'gaming relationship' is quite stable. However, there is certainly room for clarity and more overstanding. Your effort is there, we just need to *power it up* a bit. Your child enjoys this experience, trust in that positive thought and continue to be open to building a stronger relationship.

60-69 - You communicate with your child and there is some representation of overstanding. However, you probably have frustrating moments as it pertains to your child and their 'gaming relationship'. There is certainly room for relationship building. Continue reading for more insight. Your 'gaming relationship' is not as stable, but there is certainly room for growth and clarity. You've got this, keep pressing. Your child is yearning for your deeper involvement and you are too. Keep pressing for this relationship growth, it is worth it.

50-59 - You may be experiencing some frustration as it pertains to your child and the 'gaming relationship'. These frustrations may not be overwhelming, but they are certainly present. I am so excited about your connection to my book and look forward to your progress! Please continue to strive, if you don't intervene and seek to foster your relationship with your child, it could get overwhelming. Press for a more fruitful 'gaming relationship' with your child. You are not too far off! You've got this. It may feel uncomfortable at first, but you can do this. The space and emptiness you feel can be filled with positive experiences and key moments. Keep reading and be sure to dive deep, you'll see!

40-49 - My oh my, I know where you are at this exact moment. You are beyond slightly frustrated. It is imperative that you intervene. This reference guide will certainly help you build your 'gaming relationship' with your child. Press for a more fruitful experience. It may feel uncomfortable at first, but you've got this and I promise it is worth it. The space and emptiness you feel can be filled with positive experiences and memorable moments. Decide to do the work, plan out your experience, use the resources and press! Take your time and digest this guide. Believe in yourself, you and your gamer are worth the *deep dive*! (Note: If you need to, jump to Level Seven, and focus on those Team Affirmations that have been written for you)!

30-39 - The time, where does it go right? It seems like your child can play the game FOREVER. Hours and hours can go by, but you and your child rarely have healthy conversations. Your child won't stop to connect with family and there seems to be a huge wedge in between you and your child. Your 'gaming relationship' is suffering and there is definite room for improvement. I get it, and I overstand. Guess what?! There is hope!!! Keep reading, keep processing, keep trying, and keep praying. Your overall relationship with your child will get better. Try using one tip or tool that may have an impact to help to boost your morale. This entire process may feel uncomfortable at first, but you've got this and I promise it is worth it. The space and emptiness you feel can be filled with positive experiences and key moments. Keep reading and be sure to dive deep, you'll see! (Note: If you need to, jump to Level Seven, and focus on those Team Affirmations that have been written for you)!

20-29 - You are truly yearning for help, but it almost seems as if your child is only peaceful when playing the game (while you are miserable). You are miserable and are trying to figure out how to connect with your child. You are tired of the yelling from the game room and the frustration your child sometimes feels from playing the game with others. These spaces can be draining because you are frustrated too. I know how you feel as the parent/guardian. I certainly was lost prior to practicing the things I am going to help you implement.

Hours and hours can go by, but you and your child rarely have healthy conversations. Your child won't stop to connect with family and there seems to be a huge wedge in between you and your child. Your 'gaming relationship' is suffering and there is definite room for improvement. I get it, and I overstand. Guess what?! There is hope!!! I am already proud of you. Keep reading, keep processing, keep trying and keep praying. Your overall relationship with your child will get better. This entire process may feel uncomfortable at first, but you've got this and I promise it is worth it. The space and emptiness you feel can be filled with positive experiences and key moments. Choose one tool or a few Light-bulb Questions to start, you will be surprised by the response you get. Your gamer wants this healthy interaction as well. Keep reading and be sure to dive deep, you'll see! (Note: If you need to, jump to Level Seven, and focus on those Team Affirmations that have been written for you)!

10-19 - You are stagnant, please know you're not alone. I have had so many conversations with a plethora of people who were in the same place. This is a concern of many. It almost seems as if your child is only peaceful when playing the game (while you are miserable). You are miserable trying to figure out how to connect with your child. You are tired of the yelling from the kitchen and living room. The frustration your child sometimes feels from playing the game with others, the emotions and the *game life* can be baffling. This situation doesn't help because you are frustrated too. You are thinking… If this frustrates my child so much, why are they playing? Why don't they just log off and stop playing? Questions such as these may begin to saturate your mind. I know how you feel as the parent/guardian. I extremely lost prior to practicing what I am going to encourage you to practice!

Hours and hours can go by with your child and their *'time on game'*, but you and your child can't seem to have a healthy conversation without their face being buried in their phone (or on the game). Your child won't stop to connect with family at all, it is almost like they go missing and there seems to be a huge wedge between you and your child. Your 'gaming relationship' is suffering and there is definite room for improvement. I get it, and I overstand. Guess what?! There is hope!!! Keep reading, keep processing, keep trying and keep praying. Your overall relationship with your child will get better. Try to implement a tool or tip from the guide that feels the most relatable. It may feel uncomfortable at first, but you've got this and I promise it is worth it. The space and emptiness you feel can be filled with positive experiences and key moments. Keep reading and be sure to dive deep, you will see! (Note: If you need to, jump to Level Seven, and focus on those Team Affirmations that have been written for you)!

0-9 - You really are desperate and need assistance. You may even cry sometimes due to the overwhelming feeling this separation causes. You may have prayed too. You probably feel numb and stagnant when it comes to this situation. Please know you are not alone. I have had so many conversations with others, and this is a concern of many. It almost seems as if your child is only peaceful when playing the game (while you are miserable). So, what do you do? You let them play in order to have a little 'fake peace'.

You are trying to figure out how to connect with your child. You are tired of the yelling from the game room, the frustration your child sometimes feels from playing the game with others, the emotional rollercoaster and beyond. This situation doesn't help because you are frustrated too. I know how you feel as the parent/guardian. Trust me, I lived this life.

Hours and hours can go by, and you and your child won't attempt to have a healthy conversation. While playing the game, your child won't stop to connect with family and there seems to be a huge wedge between you and them. Their gaming activity and your levels of overstanding are worlds apart. Your 'gaming relationship' is suffering and there is great room for improvement. You have attempted to talk to your child, you talk to your friends, and your friends may have a similar concern. Guess what?! You may be able to help them and your family too. I am here to help, not because I did things perfectly, but because I made my fair share of mistakes. Trust me, I was in this score range too and slowly but surely worked my way up, you can Level Up and Win too!

 *Bonus:* *It's not how you start, it's how you finish. You've got this!*

YOUR CONFIRMATION:

The moment my pain turned into a blessing, and I realized that I couldn't be the only one with this experience, I wanted to bless others. Please *overstand* that making a direct connection with this book, myself or someone who shared this with you isn't an accident. This is an intentional experience. You have picked up this book at the perfect time. It is never too late, as a matter of fact your timing is divine. I appreciate you for letting me in the private spaces of your heart, mind, body and soul. Thank you for trusting me to help you and your gamer. Keep reading, keep processing, keep writing, keep connecting, keep doing, keep connecting and keep praying. Your overall relationship with your child will get better. Let's continue!

(Note: If you need to, jump to Level Seven, and focus on those Team Affirmations that have been written for you)! You certainly can! There are separate affirmations for you and your gamer!

IT'S ALL RELEVANT:

So, why did I have you take a quiz? Well, I wanted you to have a measurable tool that would help you see if your efforts have worked! Also, most times we need to *overstand* how goals are created and why they are important. Data is important and sometimes you won't realize how far you have come without actual data and proof. (This is also for our quantitative data junkies. I know the qualitative data will literally and figuratively tell the story).

I am proud of you, no matter what your score says, effort is so important and goes a long way!

Level 7: G.A.M.E. Mode· Affirm

Team Affirmations

Feel free to write these out and post them anywhere you'd like. I write mine on post-it notes and place them on my mirror, wall, or refrigerator! You can also take a picture and store it on your phone!

Repeat these to yourself **out loud,** at least *three* times a day. If you are unable to do this, be sure to start with once a day and build from there. Your relationship with yourself, your gamer and/or your loved ones are worth it. Happy Affirming!

Gamer (Child or Loved One who Games)	Support Person (Parent, Guardian, Significant Other, School Leader, Etc.)
I love myself and believe in my future.	I love myself and believe in my future.
I am open to welcoming others into my gaming space and gaming world.	I am meeting my Gamer where they are on their journey.
I choose to have an open mind and patient heart when communicating with others as they are attempting to *overstand* my desire for *Gaming*.	I choose to have an open mind and patient heart when communicating with my Gamer.
I am confident and capable of communicating with others who care for me.	I am confident and capable of communicating with my Child.
I practice sharing, considering others, and embracing safe spaces.	I am confident and capable of communicating with my Gamer about my thoughts and feelings.
I practice thinking outside the box and include my support system when it comes to gaming.	I practice listening, *Getting Above the Mis-Education*, and attempt to learn more about my Gamer.
I am aware of my emotions, they are important, and I care about myself.	I am aware of my emotions. I give my Gamer the space to express who they are.
I am in control of myself and my gaming time.	I allow my Gamer to play their game and expect positive outcomes.

Gamer (Child or Loved One who Games)	Support Person (Parent, Guardian, Significant Other, School Leader, Etc.)
I participate in a healthy balance of gaming and time with those I care for.	Engaging with my Gamer is important to me. I participate in a healthy balance of *gameplay* with my Gamer.
I participate in a healthy balance of gaming and spend time focusing on my educational, physical, social-emotional, and personal goals.	I am serious about 'leveling up' the relationship with my Gamer. I am dedicated to reading this book, learning more, and practicing the tips and strategies offered.
I am learning from those who care for me, and I am happily learning more about them.	I am learning more about my Gamer, and I am happily sharing my experiences.
I participate in a healthy balance of gaming and my school or career responsibilities.	I give myself grace and practice the necessary skills to build a healthy relationship with my Gamer.
I have fruitful conversations that lead to honest expression and positive outcomes.	I have fruitful conversations that lead to honest expression and positive outcomes with my Child or Gamer.
I respect myself and my relationships by monitoring my game time.	I respect myself and my relationships by monitoring the time I spend participating in hobbies of my own.

Gamer (Child or Loved One who Games)	Support Person (Parent, Guardian, Significant Other, School Leader, Etc.)
I respect my time and *overstand* that my time is valuable.	I respect my time and *overstand* that my time is valuable
I monitor my own actions and take accountability for them.	I monitor my own actions and take accountability for them.
I love myself, I believe in my future, and I value my relationships.	I love myself, I believe in my future, and I value my relationships.
I am aware that many opportunities are possible if I decide to foster a career around Gaming.	I am aware and accepting of the many opportunities and career paths that are possible for my Gamer.
I nurture my mind and make wise decisions.	I nurture my mind, and my Gamer's mind. I make wise decisions for my home and community.
I respect myself, my family, my community, and others.	I respect myself, my gamer, my community, and others.

Feel Free to Write Your Own Affirmations!

Writing your own Affirmations Guidelines:

1. Use positive words and do NOT use a negation or a negative word in your description.
2. Write in the present tense (not the past or the future). Write as if what you are affirming is in the present tense and is happening right now.
3. Visualize yourself as you write and cite the affirmation!

Your Turn! Your Level You've Got this, I believe in you!

Gamer (Child or Loved One who Games)	Support Person (Parent, Guardian, Significant Other, School Leader, Etc.)

Feel Free to Write Your Affirmations Here!

Feel Free to Write Your Affirmations Here!

Level 8: G.A.M.E. Story Mode

THE FINALE
Your Story; *Your* LEVEL

Free Write: This is *YOUR CHAPTER*

This is for you to write. I invite you to share your own thoughts. This is your reflection *level*; it is especially important to think about how this book has impacted your life.

Bonus: You can stop here and revisit this level or any other level when you need to. This is your reference tool. Make your imprint!

Be sure to keep learning, growing, and creating your narrative. Share when you have learned more and please send me your testimonies! I want to hear your testimonies, your good news, and about your journey with the person you shared this book experience with. You can share your comments on Amazon, on social media Pages, via email or through the *contact me* option on my website!

In the spaces below, write down your reflections and how your relationship with your child has progressed. Do you feel you can be more effective and impactful in your child's or gamer's life now that you have a guide to assist you through your gaming journey?

_____
_____
_____
_____
_____
_____
_____
_____
_____
_____
_____
_____
_____
_____
_____
_____
_____
_____
_____
_____
_____
_____
_____
_____
_____
_____
_____

What are your three most useful tips, tools, tips, and/or theories you implement the most with your gamer?

What can you do to ensure your relationship continues to grow from here? Write down what that looks like, sounds like, and feels like. Be sure to get as specific as possible. Specific goals are the ones we reach for, with intent and focus.

_____
_____
_____
_____
_____
_____
_____
_____
_____
_____
_____
_____
_____
_____
_____
_____
_____
_____
_____
_____
_____
_____
_____
_____
_____
_____
_____
_____

What did you notice about your engagement with the person you took this journey with? Did you learn anything about yourself you are willing to admit? If so, how can this self-realization assist you in life?

_____
_____
_____
_____
_____
_____
_____
_____
_____
_____
_____
_____
_____
_____
_____
_____
_____
_____
_____
_____
_____
_____
_____
_____
_____
_____
_____
_____
_____

I believe in you, and I am so happy for you! You did the work; you have progressed, and you have officially *gotten above the mis-education…* and you *Overstand the G.A.M.E.!*

YOU have the potential to excel in any GAME or Life Scenario… As long as you embrace LOVE, remain open to learning and strive to deeply OVERSTAND!

It is so amazing when we embrace who we are, who we are not, what works for us and what may not. We all have choices, it is okay to become human. Trust that we will be in the next phase of Overstanding the G.A.M.E. -In a new capacity and an entirely new experience. The choices we make matter… and soon, you will learn just how much. See you next time, on the Next Level of OVERSTANDING the G.A.M.E.!

Notes and Reflections

Do you have any *light-bulb moments* to share? Feel free to use this space for additional notes throughout your journey. You can write down any thoughts you may have, want to revisit, or unpack later!

Notes and Reflections

Do you have any *light-bulb moments* to share? Feel free to use this space for additional notes throughout your journey. You can write down any thoughts you may have, want to revisit, or unpack later!

_____
_____
_____
_____
_____
_____
_____
_____
_____
_____
_____
_____
_____
_____
_____
_____
_____
_____
_____
_____
_____
_____
_____
_____
_____
_____
_____

Notes and Reflections

Do you have any *light-bulb moments* to share? Feel free to use this space for additional notes throughout your journey. You can write down any thoughts you may have, want to revisit, or unpack later!

Notes and Reflections

Do you have any *light-bulb moments* to share? Feel free to use this space for additional notes throughout your journey. You can write down any thoughts you may have, want to revisit, or unpack later!

Your Story, Your Level:
Your Conclusion
Take the Post-Quiz!

POST- QUIZ:

I want you to take this quiz and answer each question honestly. This will be helpful as you assess where you are now versus when you took the pre-quiz. I hope this reference guide and your real-life application have a positive impact on your relationship and your **Post-G.A.M.E. Score.**

Answer these questions on a scale of 0-10 (0 being "I Highly Disagree" and 10 being "I Highly Agree")

1. I am familiar with the ESRB rating system _____
2. I know the names of at least three of the video games my child plays currently. _____
3. I play video games with my child _____
4. I know the names of at least two people my gamer plays video games with _____
5. There are benefits to playing the game _____
6. I can name at least five benefits or positive characteristics my child can attain from playing the game_____
7. My child and I have a great *overstanding* as it relates to their gaming activity _____
8. I engage in conversations with my child surrounding the game that help me *overstand* details pertaining to their experience. _____
9. I feel positive and at ease when my child plays the game _____
10. I am comfortable with the amount of time my child spends playing the game_____

Post-G.A.M.E. Score (New): _____

(Go to back to Level Six (6) to read the scaled results for your new score)

Next: Grab your first score from The Pre-Quiz that is in Level 6. (The one you completed in the beginning of your journey). Write your score below.

Pre-G.A.M.E. Score: _____

Let's calculate! What is the difference between your two scores? _____

Special Note: So, you have taken your Post-Quiz and you have your **Pre-G.A.M.E. Score**. Congrats! If you are taking your time and you try a few tips, practices, Light-Bulb Moments, etc. you may find that your relationship(s) are getting better, but you have not finished the book yet. If you really want to you may take the Post-Quiz before you complete the entire book. You can honestly take the Post-Quiz to assess your progress when you feel the need. (However, *I would love for you to take it after you complete the entire book to attain the greatest results and* **Post-G.A.M.E. Score**).

Bonus: Remember, if you are compelled to feel free to take the Post-Quiz and utilize this book in the manner that is most helpful to you! This is not a one size fits all tool. If there is growth and love present… AND your relationships are progressing in a positive capacity, I am grateful!

Again, you may also have some Qualitative Research experiences. This is research that "Tells the Story" and this is very fitting as well (even though it doesn't fall under a S,M.A.R.T. Goal per se). Testimonies and success stories are examples of data and evidence too!

Part 3

Resources to Guide You on Your Journey

I.	Bibliography
II.	Glossary
III.	Learning Terms
IV.	Overstanding the G.A.M.E. Theories and Practices
V.	S.M.A.R.T. Goals Summary
VI.	S.M.A.R.T. Goals Detailed Breakdown
VII.	Final Appreciation and Words
VIII.	About the Author

I. Bibliography:

A., Boyan & J., Sherry, "The Challenge in Creating Games for Education: Aligning Mental Models with Game Models," *Child Development Perspectives Vol.* 5, no. 2, (2011): 82-87.

Caroline Miller, "How to help Children Calm Down," *Child Mind Institute*, July 29 2024, https://childmind.org/article/how-to-help-children-calm-down/.

Chaarani, Bader PhD, Ortigara, Joseph MS., et al. "Association of video gaming with cognitive performance among children". *JAMA Open Network*, October 24, 2022. https://jamanetwork.com/journals/jamanetworkopen/fullarticle/.

Corso, David. "Holistic Gaming: Using the Physical and Psychological Effects of Video Games to Better Our Lives," B.S. Honors Research Fellowship Thesis, University of South Carolina, Columbia, 2013, https://sc.edu/about/offices_and_divisions/research/news_and_pubs/caravel/archive/2014/2014-caravel-video-games.php

Dan, A. "20 Interesting Facts About Jerry Lawson," *World's Facts*, May 1, 2023 https://www.worldsfacts.com/20-interesting-facts-about-jerry-lawson/#:~:text=Lawson%E2%80%99s%20parents%20were%20both%20postal%20workers,%20and%20he

Fullerton, Tracy (2014). Game Design Workshop: A Playcentric Approach to Creating Innovative Games. CRC Press. ISBN 978-1482217179.

Griffiths, Mark. "The Educational Benefits of Videogames," *Education and Health Vol. 20, no. 3 (*2022):47-51, https://sheu.org.uk/sheux/EH/eh203mg.pdf.

History Tools, "What was the Video Game Crash of 1983 and Why Did it Happen? A Comprehensive Look", *History Tools*, November, 19, 2023 https://www.historytools.org/docs/what-was-the-video-game-crash-of-1983-and-why-did-it-happen

Leonard, Kimberly, Rob Watts. "The Ultimate Guide to S.M.A.R.T. Goals" *Forbes Advisor*, July 9, 2024, The Ultimate Guide to S.M.A.R.T. Goals – Forbes Advisor

Marisa Upson, "What Is a Game Coder's Salary?,"*BC BootCamps,* April 18,2023, https://www.bestcolleges.com/bootcamps/guides/game-coders-salary/.

Moore, Michael (2011). Basics of Game Design. Taylor & Francis. ISBN 978-1568814339.

Mullen, Matt. "Video Game History," *HISTORY.com,* October 17, 2022, A&E Television Networks, https://www.history.com/topics/inventions/history-of-video-games.

Mullis, Steve "Inventor Ralph Baer, The Father of Video Games dies at 92." *All Tech Considered, Tech Culture and Connection,* December 8, 2014, Inventor Ralph Baer, The 'Father Of Video Games,' Dies At 92 : All Tech Considered : NPR

"Ohio's K-12 Social and Emotional Learning Standards," June 2019, *Department of Education & Workforce,* https://education.ohio.gov/getattachment/Topics/Learning-in-Ohio/Social-and-Emotional-Learning/K-12-SEL-Standards-Full-Final.pdf.

"Over." Merriam-Webster.com Dictionary, Merriam-Webster, https://www.merriam-webster.com/dictionary/over. Accessed 30 Aug. 2024.

"Overstand." Merriam-Webster.com Dictionary, Merriam-Webster, https://www.merriam-webster.com/dictionary/overstand. Accessed 30 Aug. 2024.

Shagan, Ethan H. "English Expansion and the Empire of Moderation." *The Rule of Moderation: Violence, Religion and the Politics of Restraint in Early Modern England.* Cambridge University Press, 2011. 187-219.

Snider, Mike. "Before Nintendo and Atari: How a Black Engineer Changed the Video Game Industry Forever." *USA Today*, February 27, 2020, https://www.usatoday.com/story/tech/2020/02/27/how-black-engineer-forever-changed-video-game-consoles/4752682002/

"Suicide Prevention: Facts About Suicide," *National Center for Injury Prevention and Control,* April 25, 2024, https://www.cdc.gov/suicide/facts/index.html.

Veronica Combs, "8 hours and 27 minutes. That's how long the average gamer plays each week," *TechRepublic,* March 10, 2021, https://www.techrepublic.com/article/8-hours-and-27-minutes-thats-how-long-the-average-gamer-plays-each-week/.

II. Glossary

This Glossary Includes the Following:

Important Gaming Terms, Learning Terms, Overstanding the G.A.M.E. Theories and Practices & S.M.A.R.T. Goals and more. This section will enhance your Gaming Experience as you use this tangible resource guide for your Overstanding!

Gaming Terms

Binge Gaming: This occurs when the game is played for long periods of time without a break or moment to step away.

Cheat Code: This is a pattern or numerical code or sequence that can be entered once a child is in the game that usually unlocks another level, fortune, a life, extra points etc.

Downloadable Content (DLC): This stands for downloadable content. Most of the time DLCs are purchased and are additions to a game. They can benefit a gamer by providing additional appearances and abilities. There are even some DLCs which may add an additional story mode.

Entertainment Software Gaming Board (ESRB): This rating system was founded by the video game industry in 1994 after consulting a wide range of child development and academic experts, analyzing other rating systems, and conducting nationwide research with parents. ESRB found that parents wanted a rating system that has both age-based categories and concise and impartial information regarding content. With this philosophy in mind, today the ESRB administers a three-part system that includes Rating Categories, Content Descriptors, and Interactive Elements.

First Person Shooter (FPS): This is the idea that a gamer has a vantage point through the eyes of the main character.

*Game IDs: These are specific names and nicknames that are created so other gamers can find and invite others to play. **Be sure to pay attention to these, these IDs can belong to people from anywhere and of any age.*

Game Phase: The period of time that a gamer starts and concludes their journey of gaming.

Game Ratings: Was a system created after the Video Game Crash of 1983 which gave consumers clarity on which games were age appropriate for their children. This new rating system was a key factor in the rise of video gaming.

Gamers: Your child and others who play different games on different platforms.

Gaming Relationship: The relationship that you have between yourself and your child. This relationship pertains to the clarity, engagement and communication that takes place between you and your child.

Health Points *(HP's or HP):* Refers to the amount of damage a character can take before they are unconscious or killed. Having an elevated level of health can help a gamer during their gaming experience.

In-Game Purchases:

Contains in-game offers to purchase digital goods or premiums with real world currency, including, but not limited to bonus levels, skins, music, virtual coins and other forms of in-game currency, subscriptions, season passes and upgrades (e.g., to disable ads).

In-Game Purchases (Includes Random Items):

Contains in-game offers to purchase digital goods or premiums with real world currency (or with virtual coins or other forms of in-game currency that can be purchased with real world currency) for which the player doesn't know prior to purchase the specific digital goods or premiums they will be receiving (e.g., loot boxes, item packs, mystery awards).

Practice: The boards and introduction that Gamers engage in prior to the real game starting. In some games this is the time that Gamers can run around and see the layout of the game while waiting on enough people to join.

Ragequit: When a gamer instantly quits, exits, walks away and/or powers off their game due to them being upset because of what they are experiencing at that moment.

Shares Location: Includes the ability to display the user's location to other users of the app.

Skins: Are different outfits/suits that characters can wear and change throughout a game.

Solo-Ult: This is short for Solo-Ultimate. This is a particular object or move that may be used to cause damage to a group of characters when necessary.

Squads: Is another way Gamers say teams.

THE GAME: The Electronic system which hooks up to a television, screen, laptop, or phone that includes characters, strategy, and a competitive platform. This system has acquired a great deal of our children's time, energy, and mental capacity. They can spend their time engaging and playing in solitude or with others.

Time on Game: The amount of time your child spends on the game.

Unrestricted Internet:

Provides unrestricted access to the internet (e.g., browser, search engine)

Users Interact: Indicates possible exposure to unfiltered/uncensored user-generated content, including user-to-user communications and media sharing via social media and networks. (Be mindful, your Gamer may have the ability to connect with people from all over the world).

"**Can I get on**": This is how Gamers ask if they can play the game with another Gamer who is already playing.

"**He's On Me**" This means an enemy is attacking or coming close to the character.

"**I'm Him**": - This is said by a gamer when the person has done something well and is giving kudos and/or accolades to themselves.

"**No Cap**" You may hear your Gamer saying this when they are telling the truth and whatever is happening or said is real.

III. Learning Terms

Productive Struggle: Is the time and space allotted for a child or person to press through their critical thinking strategies as they develop answers to questions and find solutions.

Relationship Skills: The abilities to establish and maintain healthy and supportive relationships and to effectively navigate settings with diverse individuals and groups. This includes the capacities to communicate clearly, listen actively, cooperate, work collaboratively to problem solve and negotiate conflict constructively, navigate settings with differing social and cultural demands and opportunities, provide leadership, and seek or offer help when needed.

Responsible Decision-Making: The abilities to make caring and constructive choices about personal behavior and social interactions across diverse situations. This includes the capacity to consider ethical standards and safety concerns, and to evaluate the benefits and consequences of various actions for personal, social, and collective well-being.

Teachable Moment: A specific point in time when an individual is most receptive to learning something. It is based on the idea that information learned during a specific period, when an individual is faced with a problem or opportunity, is more likely to be absorbed and retained.

Theory of Parental Involvement: Children whose parents or parental figures are involved in their education will be more likely to develop a strong, positive sense of efficacy for successfully achieving school-related tasks than will children whose parents are not involved.

Self-Awareness: The abilities to understand one's own emotions, thoughts, and values and how they influence behavior across contexts. This includes capacities to recognize one's strengths and limitations with a well-grounded sense of confidence and purpose.

Self-Management: The abilities to meet and achieve one's personal goals. *Fearlessness* and *Confidence* help us develop in this space. This core competency impacts the way we handle stress and navigate our internal risk and reward system, also known as our motivations. This includes the capacities to be authentic regarding one's feelings, thoughts, and behavior. It also includes the capacities to be authentic and to adjust when needed.

Social Awareness: The ability to understand the perspectives of and empathize with others, including those from diverse backgrounds, cultures, and contexts. This includes the capacities to feel compassion for others and to understand broader historical and social norms. This understanding includes behaviors represented in different settings, and recognizes family, school, community resources and other supports.

Social and Emotional Learning (SEL): is an integral part of education and human development. SEL is the process through which all young people and adults acquire and apply the knowledge, skills, and attitudes to develop healthy identities, manage emotions and achieve personal and collective goals, feel, and show empathy for others, establish and maintain supportive relationships, and make responsible and caring decisions.

IV. Overstanding the G.A.M.E. Theories/Practices/Terms:

Bonus:

An extra thought or idea given to help you *overstand* and BOOST your disposition forcing you to LEVEL UP!

Covid-19 Blur:

A time period that seems to be difficult to recall due to the *loss* track of time during the Covid-19 Pandemic.

Duo-Discovery Moments Theory:

This is the experience that both a child and a parent, guardian, or school leader can learn from each other. The communication and play are learning spaces for both members and discoveries are internalized.

Gamedates:

Time that is set aside for fully engaged gaming activities between the gamer and their parent, guardian, and/or supporter.

'Game Break Day':

Although we use the word *break*, these are actually days when your gamer should not play the game at all. Your gamer takes a complete break from engaging with anything pertaining to games. "***Game Break Day***" may be necessary because your gamer has gotten upset over the game; perhaps they are frustrated because they are not playing as well, or maybe it is just time to take a break.

Gameplay:

Gameplay is the overall experience a gamer engages in while on the game.

Gamer Meeting Theory:

The act of gamers meeting people from around the world and it being a pen pal opportunity. The difference is that it is immediate communication, and it is verbal versus the originally written process. Gamers can meet from all over the world and play the game together.

***Instant Virtual Pen-Pal**:

In this *day and age*, it is easier for children to meet others from another city, state, and country. Communication during gameplay doesn't have boundaries or wait time. The response time now is almost immediate. <u>Be sure to monitor your gamers accounts if their age is in question.</u>

Interactive Reflections:

Areas provided for the reader to give them space to share their thoughts, answers and experiences discovered as they seek to overstand the G.A.M.E.

Keys/Cheat Codes:

There are various Cheat Codes throughout this guide. Cheat codes are put in place to catapult you to higher levels during gameplay. When you see a Cheat Code in the text, be ready to level up in your overstanding and pay attention to key words and information. The information is connected to the positive characteristics and benefits gamers can learn and internalize while playing. These are the building blocks that will help them as they progress through life. These Keys are also detrimental as it pertains to their Social-Emotional Learning foundation and overall growth. <u>There are sections where the *Keys* and *Cheat Codes* mirror one another to reiterate the significance of the Social Emotional Learning Focus.</u>

Light-Bulb Moments/Questions:

Are highlighted sections set to encourage healthy communication and intentional interactions between a person and their gamer. These *moments* seek to inspire relationship building experiences, conversation starters, critical thinking tools and stimulate cognitive creativity.

Main Character Energy:

The idea of a gamer owning their skills, resources and abilities taken from the game and executing this confidence during *gameplay* and in real life (*IRL*).

'Minute for Minute' Theory:

This is a practice I created to help my Gamer overstand the true concept of a minute. Instead of just agreeing to let your child play the game, you can create a **Game Bank**. This is a place where they will *earn* and *save* time, so they are able to play the game. They can earn time by doing chores, reading, engaging with family etc. Your child will earn a minute of play for every minute they engage in other productive activities. (Hence the name, "Minute for Minute.' The accountability factor is exercised during this process.

It is an immensely helpful tool because you can negotiate time and Game Bank Minutes. Ex: If I needed a little extra help around the house, I'd say, "Son, I'll add 30 minutes to your Game Bank if you help me with this task." He'd almost always agree! This strategy has been one of the key strategies executed throughout our experience. It helps him stay on a schedule, monitor his own *gameplay* and it has helped him process the true meaning of a minute (because when he is playing, the concept of time feels different).

The Energy Awareness Theory:

We sometimes get caught off guard because we don't know where certain energy is coming from. We need to feel where the energy is coming from to comprehend the source. Parents and guardians should be conscious of their energy when engaging with their child. Ex: What kind of mood are you in prior to addressing your child regarding their *time on game*. It is important for parents/guardians/school leaders to be aware of their personal space and the feeling inside of them.

The 'I Wasn't Like That' Theory:

The idea that Parents/Guardians overstand what children experience because of their experience and thoughts related to playing the game. Times are different, social media and technology have rearranged our world. Attempt *overstanding the* G.A.M.E. and process this unique way of thinking.

The Intentional Engagement Theory:

The idea that creating a space to be involved in your child's life is necessary. This *time* is planned and scheduled. The idea behind this engagement is meaningful, purposeful, and rooted in love.

Theory of Parental Involvement Regarding Gaming:

Children whose parents/guardians are involved in their child's gaming experiences will be more likely to build a stronger, more positive sense of overstanding, peace, and efficacy as it relates to their child.

Theory of Parental Involvement Regarding Gaming and Beyond:

Children whose parents/guardians are involved in their child's gaming, extra-curricular activities, desires and points of interest will be more likely to build a stronger, more positive sense of overstanding, peace, and efficacy as it relates to their child.

The Productive Struggle of Gaming Theory:

This is the time offered to a gamer which allows them to press for a goal when it may not be easy to do so. In this moment, allowing time for the gamer to figure it out is pertinent. Granting them the opportunity and space to discover an answer on their own will help them develop problem solving skills. This answer may not be 100 percent correct. However, the critical thinking process, current experience and prior knowledge will help build their confidence and is a bright spot to look forward to.

Bonus Definition for OVERstanding the G.A.M.E.:

This is the place where my Sun wants me to tell you to, "Read the Book." :)

V. S.M.A.R.T. Goals Summary

As an educator of 25+ years, I have grown to love the S.M.A.R.T. goal measurement system. In order to have proper goals they must be **Specific**. Having a particular goal is important so you will know when you have reached this very specific goal. Making it too broad will not help and can become frustrating if you don't know what you are actually trying to accomplish. The next step is to make sure it is **Measurable**!

I am certain that you will show growth in your relationship and in points. **Attainable** is the next step and of course your goal is attainable. You have to set out the necessary time to dedicate towards reading, reflecting and engaging with your child. I know you purchased this reference guide because you want progress! You've got this! **Relevant**, oh my, let's see… Is gaming relevant today? It sure is. Let's consider a deeper level of relevance.

Is your relationship with your child important and relevant? It most certainly is! I am sure your core value system is grounded in your desire to create and build an everlasting relationship with your child and gamer. Lastly, your goal must be **Time-Bound**. This means there should be a plan for when you want this goal to be fully executed and complete. This time frame is solely up to you. You can schedule and plan with this reference guide and the suggestions, so they fit your life. I believe we must do what works for our family unit and set up. We don't have "cookie cutter" lives nor experiences. So, prior to starting, I hope you took some time to think, pray and meditate on what this journey might look like for you!

VI. SMART Goals Intricately Defined

(Just in Case You Want More Depth)

A S.M.A.R.T. Goal is defined by its five key aspects or elements. Without all aspects, you might be goal setting but not effectively creating a plan for success. Let's look at the five elements of S.M.A.R.T. Goals.

Specific

Specific goals have a desired outcome that is clearly understood. No matter what it is, the goal should be clearly articulated so that everyone is on the same page with the objective. Define what will be accomplished and the actions to be taken to accomplish the goal.

Measurable

These are the numbers used with the goal. You need to have a quantifiable objective so that you can track progress. Define what data will be used to measure the goal and set a method for collection.

Achievable

Goals need to be realistic to maintain the enthusiasm to try to achieve them. Setting lofty goals is good, but you may want to break them down into smaller, bite-sized chunks. If the goal is not doable, you may need to first ramp up resources to give yourself a shot at success. (Ramping up resources would be its own S.M.A.R.T. Goal).

Relevant

Goals should be aligned with the desires of those involved. Don't set goals just as an exercise for something to do. One way to determine if the goal is relevant is to define the key benefit to the person(s).

Time-Bound

Goals should have a deadline. A goal without a deadline does not do much. How can you identify success or failure? This is why S.M.A.R.T. Goals set a final date. This doesn't mean that all the work is done, but it means that you can evaluate the success of the endeavor and set new goals.

Benefits of S.M.A.R.T. Goals

There are a lot of benefits to setting S.M.A.R.T. Goals, which is why you should consider adding them to your toolbox. First, a S.M.A.R.T. Goal helps to give you an objective. In doing this, you can identify strengths and weaknesses. Second, a S.M.A.R.T. Goal provides motivation to succeed. When you know where the goal line is, you'll want to work to meet or beat it. Third, a good S.M.A.R.T. Goal, while attainable, will also be challenging and force you out of your comfort zone. Ultimately, the S.M.A.R.T. Goal is a useful tool to remain focused on attaining a goal.

Basic Example of S.M.A.R.T. Goal

Overstanding the G.A.M.E. Goals:

"I'm going to have a better relationship with my gamer."

Specific: "I am going to learn more about myself and my gamer and invest in this relationship by using this book as a resource. I will put in the time to ensure we are in a better space as it relates to the game."

Measurable: "I am going to take the Pre-Quiz and complete the reading, activities, and the work. Then, I will take the Post-Quiz and my goal is to have a 30% increase as it pertains to our relationship."

Achievable: "I can afford to purchase Overstanding the G.A.M.E., and I believe my gamer and I can accomplish this goal (if we do the work)."

Relevant: "I want to build my relationship with my gamer. I really miss connecting with them."

Time-bound: "I will pull out my planner tomorrow and plan to review the book to learn more about the levels in the guide. I will take the Pre-Test this week and I will set aside time to pour into this goal each day with the ultimate goal being that we are in a better space within 45 days (3/24/2025)."

How To Follow Through on Your Goals

What is the use of having a goal if you aren't going to follow through with it? Once you have goals, there are a few things that you can do to ensure you stay on track and achieve them.

Write Goals Down (Feel Free to use Your Writing Tool)

Take the time to write down your goals and post them somewhere so that you can see them. For combined goals, place them somewhere where you and your gamer(s)/additional people can see them. If it's just for yourself, post a note next to your computer screen with the goals. Writing goals down brings them to life and makes them real. It's also a good reminder of what you are working on.

Bonus: You can have your S.M.A.R.T. Goals and your Team Affirmation in the same space!

Share Goals with Relevant People

Sharing goals sets the tone of accountability. Share goals with your significant other, your gamer, best friend, or a mentor. A shared goal is a goal that comes with a commitment to work hard to achieve the goal. Make sure that you share goals with a supportive person who will encourage you to press on when things get hard.

Regularly Evaluate Progress

Check in and see how you're doing toward your goal. If the goal is a monthly goal, you may want to have daily or weekly check-ins to see what progress has been made. This helps you redirect your energy and change course if something you are doing isn't working and you aren't making progress. It is better to see this sooner than later while you can still adapt and adjust in real-time with enough time to succeed.

Celebrate Wins

When you succeed, celebrate. But don't think that you need to wait until the entire goal is achieved before you give yourself a pat on the back. If you find yourself and your Gamer making excellent progress during a check-in, celebrate that too. The small wins help you maintain the energy to work toward the bigger goal.

VII. My Final Appreciation and Words for You, The Winner!

OMG! You made it to this part?! #Tears… Thank you so much for trusting me. Thank you for doing the work and for being optimistic! My mission is to pour Love into this world and impact others one person at a time. I am grateful that you are now a part of my journey too. Your WIN matters to me!

You were able to think outside of the box, move any doubts to the side, challenge yourself and LEVEL UP! There is so much information here, you may even need to read it more than once and that is perfectly okay. Feel free to revisit this guide as often as you'd like. This is your journey to leveling up with your gamer. You've got the Ultimate Cheat Code to Level Up and Win in your relationship with your Gamer!

 *Final Bonus of OTG:* *You have the potential to excel in any Game of Life scenario… As long as you embrace LOVE, remain open to learning and strive to deeply OVERSTAND!*

Congratulations you have officially completed and WON this G.A.M.E.

~Shartia 'Love' Jones, *GAME* Coach

VIII. About the Author:

Shartia 'Love" Jones is gifted in public speaking, literary writing, and motivating through education. She is the founder of, *The Love Jones Alliance Inc.*, and holds a bachelor's degree in Corporate, Interpersonal Communication, a Master's Degree in Education, and certificates in TV, Radio Broadcasting, and Life Coaching. Her gifts and degrees are more than knowledge, but personally and professionally rewarding passions. She has professionally emceed large events and hosted local television shows over the last twelve years, throughout the Chicagoland area. Ms. Jones is grateful for her communication ability and has used it to become a published author, to record voice-overs for two of Chicago's most prominent radio stations, *WGCI* and *V103* and beyond.

Shartia 'Love' Jones has combined her communications skills, education, and authentic life experiences to express the value of sharing love to the world through our divinely given gifts. Ms. Jones hopes and prays that others will utilize their confidence, power, and internal love to overcome obstacles and surpass their goals. She is rooting for our best selves!

Shartia Jones is currently pressing forward with her vision for her company, as she releases her third published work, *Overstanding the G.A.M.E. "Getting Above the Mis-Education"*. Prior to stepping away to support her son and pursue her dreams, Shartia Jones had been in the education field for twenty-six years and was the Dean of Students for an elementary school in Chicago, IL. Her vision is to help others from the inside out, utilizing a holistic approach. "Learning to love yourself completely, heart, mind, body, and soul is the true Shartia 'Love' Jones, *divine* experience."

The goal is to go beyond *Each One, Teach One*, but to extend to *Each One, Love One*. Shartia's desire is to help her growing community experience healing, cultivate their inspirations, activate continuous growth, and remain encouraged. Her hope is that those in need will practice genuine self-love and embrace their beauty while discovering their inner strength.

Shartia is the proud mother of a teenage son whom she adores. She also loves spending time with her family and close friends. When the time allots, she teaches dance fitness classes and enjoys working out. To name a few, watching movies, listening to music, reading, and writing are some of her favorite things to do. Her favorite place to travel to is Jamaica and her favorite place to visit when she is home is the serenity of Chicago's Lakefront. She secretly wants to learn to play the drums and become fluent in speaking Spanish.

Contact Information:

TheLoveJonesAlliance@gmail.com

OverstandingTheGame@gmail.com

Website:

OverstandingTheGame.com